FASHION

QUAKE

FRANCES
LINCOLN

First published in 2022 by Frances Lincoln
an imprint of The Quarto Group.
The Old Brewery, 6 Blundell Street
London, N7 9BH,
United Kingdom
T (0)20 7700 6700
www.QuartoKnows.com

© 2022 Quarto Publishing plc

A catalogue record for this book is available from
the British Library.

ISBN 978-0-7112-6744-2
Ebook ISBN 978-0-7112-6745-9

10 9 8 7 6 5 4 3 2 1

Design by Sarah Boris

Printed in China

CAROLINE YOUNG

FASHION

QUAKE

THE MOST DISRUPTIVE MOMENTS IN FASHION

INTRODUCTION

A 1966 protest by the British Society for the Protection of Mini Skirts to preserve their skirt lengths.

Fashion is a medium that can be profoundly powerful, reflecting changes in society through the adjustment of a silhouette, or by using clothing as a tool to deliver a compelling message on a T-shirt.

Not only does what we wear reveal the stories of our time, capturing changes in politics and society, such as women's increasing power after World War I, but it can also be a form of self-expression for both designer and wearer.

As part of a series that explores movements that changed the world, FashionQuake delves into fifty moments in fashion, from the twentieth century onwards, that were so radical in their concept that they shocked, inspired and provoked. Each of these moments has been game-changing. They have challenged the status quo and led to a change in direction – for example the bikini, which encapsulated a woman's right to choose what she could wear on the beach. Others have made a cultural impact, such as Marlene Dietrich flouting gender conventions in a tuxedo, Björk dressing as a white swan for the Oscars, which shifted the very concept of what could be worn on the red carpet, and Lady Gaga's meat dress, which marked a new era of fashion delivering political messages.

While nineteenth-century century designer Charles Worth is considered the first celebrity couturier, the twentieth century heralded a new phase of fashion, led by designers like Paul Poiret, Coco Chanel, Jeanne Lanvin and Jean Patou. Their innovations broke barriers and brought new freedoms for women, leading to the concept of designer as auteur, using skills in manipulating cut and shape to create pioneering designs. Elsa Schiaparelli challenged perceptions through her surrealist concepts. Cristóbal Balenciaga changed the idea of how clothing should shape a woman. Mary Quant captured the youthful countercultural movements of the 1950s and 1960s, not just with her mini-skirt, but by transforming how people shopped, with Bazaar, her hip London boutique.

In the 1990s and 2000s, new designers came to the fore, challenging our perceptions even further. Alexander McQueen was the enfant terrible who pushed boundaries and Hussein Chalayan used technical mastery to transfix his audience. Not all were successful in their experimentations though – Marc Jacobs was sacked from Perry Ellis following the poor response to his grunge collection.

The way fashion is consumed is also ever-changing, as seen in the advent of fashion illustration and magazines in the early twentieth century, the development of the shopping experience aimed at the youth audience, the rise of fast fashion, aspirational images on Instagram and the viral dissemination of messages at protests, worn as slogans on clothing and skin.

Clothing is one way that people can challenge existing conventions and rebel against the dominant position on gender, class, race and sexuality. In the 1930s, Mexican-American and African-American youths used the audacious zoot suit as a refusal to be subservient or invisible; decades later hippies co-opted thrift store military finds to protest the Vietnam War and punks shocked society in

7

outrageous fashions to protest the class system. So, is it really surprising that fashion designers have frequently looked to street style for inspiration? Some, like Vivienne Westwood and Katharine Hamnett, have been at the forefront of this resistance fashion.

FashionQuake provides a chronological overview of the most radical, impactful moments of fashion, and features the designers and style leaders who have pushed buttons in what they wear, whether it be Madonna in her Jean Paul Gaultier-designed conical bras or Janelle Monáe in a pair of 'vagina' pants.

Broken up into five chapters, the first explores a new era in social history with Modernism and Liberation, as society changes at a rapid pace and women fight for new freedoms in how they live and what they wear. Chapter Two looks at Mid-Century Style, as fashion becomes big business and straddles the Depression era, wartime utility of World War II and post-war prosperity. Chapter Three examines the Rise of Counterculture, following the increasing visibility of the teenager and a new sense of youthful rebellion, when style shaped on the street filters into fashion. The 1980s and 1990s, marking a new era in fashion consumerism, led by Gen X and Y, is reviewed in Chapter Four. And finally, Chapter Five, Protest and Resistance, delves into how social media has pushed fashion into the hands of influencers, and how it can reflect political concerns, through larger movements such as #MeToo and Black Lives Matter (BLM).

Fashion should not be dismissed as a frivolous business solely concerned with vanity – it can shake up traditions and lead the charge when it comes to change and social transformation. This book explores the radical and pioneering fashions and their impact from the beginnings of the twentieth century.

'FASHION IS PART OF THE DAILY AIR AND IT CHANGES ALL THE TIME, WITH ALL THE EVENTS. YOU CAN EVEN SEE THE APPROACHING OF A REVOLUTION IN CLOTHES. YOU CAN SEE AND FEEL EVERYTHING IN CLOTHES.'

DIANA VREELAND

Alexander McQueen's spring–summer 2001 collection.

INTRODUCTION

MODERNISM
AND
LIBERATION

1890–1930

Never was there a period in history that heralded as much change as the first decades of the twentieth century. It marked the end of the Victorian era, with its stiff moral values, and welcomed the dawn of a new society under British King Edward VII. A time of economic growth, new technological discoveries and a more permissive society, dress reformers sought to free women from the cumbersome clothing of previous decades, as suffragettes campaigned for women to have the right to vote in order to have some political agency and parity.

A CHANGING AESTHETIC

The business of fashion underwent remarkable developments during this time. In the 1860s, Charles Worth became the first celebrity couturier, helping to launch dressmaking as an international industry. Following Worth's death, in 1895, Paul Poiret took over his fashion house, going on to form his own maison de couture in 1903. He brought a unique and impactful aesthetic to fashion, shaping innovations in how women would dress over the next decade. He sought to free women from corsets with his loose tunics, inspired by those worn by women in the Middle East, the fairytale erotica of *The Arabian Nights* and the Japanese kimono. Similarly, Lady Duff Gordon's slit-skirts and gowns, which required much less corsetry, made her the go-to designer for liberal upper-class women.

In 1910, Coco Chanel opened her first milliner's shop in Paris. Over the next decade, including the war period, she would expand into freedom-giving couture, reshaping the silhouette for active, working women. She said, 'One world was ending, another was about to be born ... an opportunity beckoned, I took it.' Chanel was not only pioneering in her approach to business – she used more accessible jersey knits for her couture – but in securing her fortune when she introduced one of the first designer perfumes, No 5, in 1921.

World War I changed everything though – not only wiping out a generation of young men and bringing thousands of women into the workforce, but provoking a sense of carpe diem, seizing the day, in the next generation and revolutionising how they dressed. Men embodied a dandy style of self-expression, while women chose to wear easy chemise dresses for dancing and playing sports, such as the innovative outfit designed by Jean Patou for tennis player Suzanne Lenglen, the star of Wimbledon in 1921.

The Roaring Twenties signalled a new phase in fashion, with magazines like the American-based *Vogue* launching international editions in the UK (1916) and France (1920). These featured illustrations that captured the modern woman drinking and smoking, and promoted avant-garde movements that fused together art, photography and fashion. While *Vogue* was aimed at wealthy women, other periodicals featured dress patterns for less affluent women to make their own versions of the latest couture at home.

The first decades of the twentieth century also saw a growth in department stores, offering a centralized place for women to buy dresses, hats, gloves and cosmetics under one roof. American businessman Harry Selfridge, realizing that British shops didn't have the glamour of US department stores like Marshall Field's, opened his magnificent new store in Oxford Street in March 1909. It not only boldly introduced a new shopping experience, but combined with societal changes, ensured that fashion would be democratised and accessible to all.

'ONE WORLD WAS ENDING, ANOTHER WAS ABOUT TO BE BORN. I WAS IN THE RIGHT PLACE; AN OPPORTUNITY BECKONED, I TOOK IT'.

COCO CHANEL

1892
→ Fashion bible *Vogue* magazine is founded in the United States.

1901
→ The death of Queen Victoria heralds the new Edwardian era under King Edward VII in Britain.

1903
→ Emmeline Pankhurst founds the Women's Social and Political Union (WSPU) to campaign for women's suffrage.

1909
→ Selfridges department store on London's Oxford Street is opened by American businessman Harry Gordon Selfridge.

1909
→ French designer Jeanne Lanvin begins selling couture to wealthy patrons.

1910
→ French Paul Poiret introduces his controversial hobble skirt, followed by his harem pants, in 1911, with the aim of reinventing female fashion. Coco Chanel opens her first hat shop at 21 rue Cambon, Paris.

1914
→ Following the outbreak of World War I, women are mobilised to the labour force, taking on jobs previously held by men, as part of the war effort.

1916
→ The British edition of *Vogue* magazine is launched.

1918
→ Following four years of devastating war, armistice is announced.
→ In the UK, women over the age of 30, who meet certain property qualifications, win the right to vote. All men over 21 are given the right to vote under the same legislation.

1920
→ The French edition of *Vogue* magazine hits the newsstands. Wimbledon women's tennis champion Suzanne Lenglen shocks crowds by wearing an innovative knee-length tennis dress by French designer Jean Patou.

1920

→ The Nineteenth Amendment is ratified in the US, granting women the right to vote.

1921

→ American writer F. Scott Fitzgerald publishes his short story collection, *Flappers and Philosophers*.

→ Chanel launches her signature perfume, No 5, as one of the first celebrity designer perfumes.

1922

→ Italian couturier Elsa Schiaparelli creates her first knitwear designs.

→ British archaeologist Howard Carter's discovery of Pharaoh Tutankhamun's tomb in the Valley of the Kings leads to a vogue for ancient Egyptian-influenced decoration.

1924

→ British outfitters Burberry introduces its signature check lining to its popular trench coats.

1925

→ The International Exhibition of Modern Decorative and Industrial Arts is held in Paris.

→ African-American diva Josephine Baker arrives in Paris to perform on stage.

→ Madeleine Vionnet opens her ready-to-wear fashion house on Fifth Avenue, New York.

1926

→ Chanel's Little Black Dress is hailed by American *Vogue* as the equivalent of the Ford motorcar in terms of functionality.

1929

→ The Wall Street Crash marks the beginning of the ten-year Great Depression in the United States.

1930

→ German actress Marlene Dietrich arrives in Hollywood.

CYCLING INTO MODERNITY

THE DIVIDED SKIRT
LADY HARBERTON
1897

In 1876, such was the taboo around women daring to wear trousers that *The New York Times* described them as 'hysterical' and 'suffering' from a 'nervous disorder'. Not only did trousers reveal the supposedly shocking shape of a woman's legs, but they were seemingly so gender identity-fixed that a woman in trousers was seen as 'unnatural'. It wasn't until the end of the nineteenth century that a practical bifurcated garment was introduced for women, mainly due to the invention and popularity of the bicycle.

Women in the Middle East had been wearing trousers for centuries, in the form of the harem-style of baggy pantaloons, but Western society was tortoise paced in catching up. In 1851, Quaker and dress reformist Amelia Bloomer led a short-lived revolution in a new practical garment based on the Turkish style of trouser. So-called 'Bloomers' quickly caught on that year, and it became common to see sketches of women in voluminous pants splashed across newspapers, portrayed as a revolutionary fashion for them. Lauded by well-known social reformers like Elizabeth Smith Miller and Susan B. Anthony, these outfits were promoted for their apparent health benefits. Satirical magazines like *Punch* took enormous delight in mocking them in cartoons in which gender reversal seemed to be a theme – women in bloomers seen acting, speaking and smoking like men, while the latter were left literally holding the babies. After reaching peak popularity in Europe in 1851, bloomers fell out of fashion and the crinoline swept back into women's wardrobes.

It was Florence Wallace Pomeroy, Viscountess Harberton, who fully promoted divided skirts, inspired by the bloomer style. In April 1881, Lady Harberton announced herself as president of the newly founded Rational Dress Society, speaking out for the increasing numbers of women who wished to have an active life but were expected to play sports in restrictive skirts and bustles. She described the perfect outfit as having freedom of movement, grace and beauty, comfort and convenience, and being light, while also offering warmth. Soon her name would lend itself to a movement of 'Harbertoners', who wore the style of divided skirts she advocated for sports and even to dances. It would be the bicycle though, which opened up new possibilities in terms of sport and travelling to work for women, that secured the bifurcated skirt's staying power.

The rapidly growing popularity for cycling among women prompted a rash of articles on what they should wear. When Lady Harberton was photographed on

Demonstrating the bicycle and a tweed cycling outfit in 1890, Chicago.

MODERNISM AND LIBERATION 1890–1930

her bicycle wearing a short, divided skirt, with a natty mutton-sleeved jacket and bow tie, Harbertoners rejoiced. Others looked on with disgust. Taken at a gathering at London's Hyde Park Corner for the Rational Dress Society's 1897 ride to Oxford, ladies were greeted by a crowd who, according to the *Daily Mail*, subjected them to misogynistic insults, such as: 'Is that your brother or the missus?', and 'You're out in your husband's things again are yer, while he's at home minding the baby?' Despite support from prominent figures like dramatist Oscar Wilde, Lady Harberton's cycling outfit was ultimately dismissed as a novelty, ridiculed for its 'masculine coldness' in *Punch*.

However Lady Harberton encouraged other women to create their own divided skirt outfits. At a time when it was almost unheard of for women to take part in extreme sports, a number of pioneering female mountaineers chose to adopt it. As one of the first women to climb Mont Blanc, Henriette d'Angeville dressed in tweed knickerbockers for the expedition. When climbing in the Alps, Irish mountaineer Lizzie Le Blond, the first president of the Ladies' Alpine Club, in 1907, chose to wear breeches under a detachable skirt, which she could whip on and off when required.

It was the necessities of World War I that finally freed women from long skirts and corsets. When it came to women stepping up as vital munitions workers, factory managers were insistent that they work safely and dresses just didn't cut it. They wore trousers and overalls, just as men had done before they'd gone to war. While that continued during World War II and more women wore trousers in the post-war period, the fight that women like Lady Harberton took on in order for women to wear trousers continues. It's hard to believe that it was only in 2016 that airline British Airways changed its mandatory rule that female cabin crew wear skirts.

'THE RATIONAL DRESS SHOULD BE ADOPTED BY ALL MOTHERS WHO WISH THEIR GIRLS TO GROW UP HEALTHY AND HAPPY.'

CONSTANCE WILDE

By 1910, French couturier Paul Poiret was shaking up couture with his designs that looked to Persia and Japan for his harem-style pants and kimono tunics, in an appropriated fashion that became known as Orientalism. The phenomenon of the Ballets Russes, a Russian dance company led by Sergei Diaghilev, also helped shape a new Modernist ethos, which incorporated art, fashion and literature to explore a new way of looking at the world.

Following the devastation felt across Europe by World War I, new forms of expression came into the fore. The traditions of old were replaced by a fresh, youthful vision. Fashions borrowed from the new art movements that marked this exciting period. Paris was the artistic centre of the Roaring Twenties, pulsating with the creative freedom found in the city, due, in part, to the mixing of different groups – Russian exiles who had escaped the 1918 Revolution, artists like Pablo Picasso and Jean Cocteau, who explored Cubism and Futurism, and hedonistic American writers like F. Scott Fitzgerald and Ernest Hemingway.

In 1925, Paris held the International Exhibition of Modern Decorative and Industrial Arts, and it was here that the concept of art deco was shaped. This would have a phenomenal impact on design over the next decade, as seen in architecture, with streamlined, Modernist skyscrapers like the Empire State Building and fashion, with geometry, elegance and Eastern influences making their appearance, including Egyptian hieroglyphics, inspired by Howard Carter's discovery of Tutankhamun's tomb in 1922.

HOBBLING INTO THE MODERN AGE

THE HOBBLE SKIRT
PAUL POIRET
1910

Paul Poiret may have been known for his freedom-giving designs, such as his loose harem pants based on Turkish trousers, but one of his most divisive credits was for the controversial hobble skirt, so tight against the legs that it limited the wearer to taking only tiny steps. The hobble was à la mode from 1910 to 1914, at a time when the Suffragists were not only trying to reform dress, but to gain rights for women.

The hobble skirt was inspired by Mrs Edith Hart O. Berg, the first American woman to fly in a passenger plane, when she took part in a 1908 Wright brothers demonstration in Le Mans, France. To ensure her skirt didn't blow up in the wind, she bound it against her legs with rope. Poiret claimed credit for the style when he introduced his first tubular skirt design in 1910, based on the narrow, high-waisted gowns of ancient Greece. The name of the skirt came from the shackles used to restrain horses by binding their front legs together. 'Yes, I freed the bust but I shackled the legs,' he said. While the skirt was restrictive, the shape of the dress required less structure underneath, with lampshade tunics or short jackets worn over the dress to help provide greater comfort.

The New York Times, in January 1912, credited the hobble skirt as a reaction against women being too active with the new dance crazes: 'the narrow skirt is having a good effect on the carriage of young women ... for it is more than grotesque to see the girls of to-day doing the turkey trot, the Argentine Tango and the grizzly bear'.

The skirt's restrictions were to prove dangerous, however, giving fuel to critics. At the Chantilly Racecourse, in September 1910, a woman in a hobbled skirt fractured her skull and later died, after a horse bolted into the crowd. Almost a year later, a hobble skirt-clad, 18-year-old Ida Goyette stumbled over a locked gate while crossing a bridge over a canal in New York State; she fell into the water and drowned. As well as the danger posed by the design, women who wore the skirt were frequently ridiculed in the press and satirized in cartoons, particularly *Punch*, often scathing of what it deemed women's frivolous fashions.

The popularity of the skirt waned with the outbreak of World War I, as its impracticality was a hamper to the work women were drafted in to do in place of men. Its legacy is evident in one of the most iconic designs of the twentieth century, the curved and fluted Coke bottle.

A 1912 French fashion illustration of a hobble skirt designed by Paquin.

CHANGES TO WOMEN'S DRESS

In the first decades of the twentieth century, women's dress underwent revolutionary change, shifting from clothing that reinforced women as dependents in their restrictive, ornamental clothing, to a style that reflected a new place for women in society.

Despite a drive for dress reform in the 1850s, with the short-lived introduction of the bloomer, by 1860 the crinoline skirt was back in fashion, and wider than ever. Female fashions were outrageously elaborate, as middle-class women became a force of consumerism, keeping up with the novelties set by royal fashion leaders Queen Victoria and Empress Eugenie.

They transformed themselves into birds of paradise in brilliantly-hued fabrics in the new synthetic colours that were all the rage, following the discovery of the first aniline dye, 'mauveine', in 1856. By the turn of the century, the silhouette for women had narrowed from the full crinolines to a desirable S-shape silhouette, achieved through corsetry and padding. Dress reform champions were also encouraging innovations such as the 'health corset', which was less rigid, and women embraced the more practical style of shirtwaist blouses, skirts and tweeds, which were adaptable for wearing when taking part in sporting activities, such as cycling and golf. This new look was immortalised by the Gibson Girl of the 1910s, an archetype of the free-spirited modern woman, as created by illustrator Charles Dana Gibson. She was defined by her hourglass figure and her active outlook; the prevalent style for a new era.

While women's fashions were slowly becoming more practical, it was the challenges of World War I that instigated major changes in how women dressed. Hundreds of thousands of women took on work in factories, munitions plants and on farms, to replace the men who were overseas. To ensure their safety in often dangerous conditions they wore similar clothing as the men, with overalls, trousers, caps and boots.

When America entered the conflict in 1917, the Women's Motor Corps of America was one of the new voluntary organisations that allowed women to participate in the war. Civilian skirts were raised six

Celebrated 'Gibson Girl' Camille Clifford showcasing the fashionable silhouette in 1906.

inches off the ground for ease of movement on public transport and for climbing into motorcars, dresses became looser and less restrictive, and women were also given pockets for the first time; one of a number of practical innovations borrowed from male clothing. Once the war was over, women were reluctant to give up the new autonomy they had found through work and in dress. The ruination of the war was not only a factor in granting women the right to vote in Britain in 1918, but it sparked a new way of dressing for women, with comfort, freedom and functionality in mind.

THE MAD MUSE

MARCHESA LUISA CASATI'S 'QUEEN OF THE NIGHT' DRESS
LÉON BAKST AND CHARLES WORTH
1922

Described as the Lady Gaga of the early twentieth century, Marchesa Luisa Casati sought to transform herself into a living work of art. She used costume as a mode of expression in inventive ways, and her 'Queen of the Night' dress, specially created for her by Léon Bakst, a fashion visionary who designed for Diaghilev's Ballets Russes, was the pinnacle of her eccentric theatricality.

She was born in Milan in 1881 as Luisa Amman to a wealthy textile manufacturer. Her parents, who both died when she was in her teens, left her a huge inheritance with which she established herself as a socialite and artist's muse. In 1900, she married Camillo, Marquess Casati Stampa di Soncino. Although they were legally separated in 1914, she used her title for the rest of her life. Travelling around Europe in the 1910s, Casati commissioned designers, such as Mariano Fortuny and Léon Bakst in Venice, and Paul Poiret in Paris. In 1920, Poiret created an exquisite fountain dress for her, with tiers of cascading pearls.

One of the most striking creations was Bakst's 'Queen of the Night' costume, a celestial fantasy aimed at turning the wearer into the living embodiment of light. Bakst sketched it for Casati to wear to a Paris Opera Ball in 1922. It featured a towering headdress covered in stars and diamond-studded netting, with tentacles of stars erupting from her body. She commissioned Parisian designer Charles Worth to bring it to life: it was so elaborate that it took over three months and 20,000 francs to construct. Casati used belladonna eyedrops to make her eyes shine, adding to the dazzling, ethereal impact of the gown.

Casati was as infamous for her costumes as she was for her parties at her palazzo on Venice's Grand Canal. She kept an exotic menagerie, including macaws and cheetahs, and performed Persian dances to guests. She was rumoured to have attended the Paris Opera wearing a headdress of peacock feathers and with fresh chicken's blood smeared on one arm, and attended parties with live snakes as necklaces. She was often seen walking her pet cheetahs around the Venice's Piazza San Marco at night, her pale skin, hennaed hair and heavily kohled eyes creating an otherworldly impression.

Casati's embodiment of spectacle and artistry aroused creativity long after her death. Elsa Schiaparelli's granddaughter, Marisa Berenson, was photographed by Cecil Beaton as the Marchesa for the famous Rothschild Ball in 1971. She also served as inspiration for Dior's spring/summer 1998 collection, Alexander McQueen's designs and Marc Jacobs' final collection for Louis Vuitton in 2013, where he brought back to life the infamous 'Queen of the Night' dress.

Marchesa Luisa Casati in the 'Queen of the Night' dress in 1922.

MODERNISM AND LIBERATION 1890—1930

THE SUFFRAGETTES

In 1908, a rally in London's Hyde Park attracted a crowd of some 300,000 people, all protesting, with their homemade banners, for the rights of women, and wearing white, purple and green, colours chosen by socialist and activist Emmeline Pethick-Lawrence to unify the movement. Purple represented loyalty and dignity, green was for hope and white symbolic of purity.

A suffrage movement had been established in 1867 in Britain, but it had had little success in achieving women's right to vote. By 1903 Emmeline Pankhurst was leading a new campaign under the Women's Social and Political Union (WSPU), which used militant tactics to ensure their voices would be heard. As they smashed windows of department stores, bombed politicians' homes and set buildings alight, they continued to be ridiculed for their supposed masculine appearance and behaviour.

Previous dress reformers, including advocates of the 'bloomer' in the 1850s, and the Rational Dress champions who'd adopted bifurcated skirts and tweed jackets for cycling, were similarly lambasted in publications like *Punch* for being too 'manly'. To off-set these criticisms and further their political cause, suffragette leaders like Pankhurst and daughter Christabel were savvy enough to realise that they should reinforce their femininity through fashion, rather than subverting it. Sylvia Pankhurst, who used her training at the Royal College of Art to shape the visuals of the WSPU, said: 'Many suffragists spend more money on clothes than they can comfortably afford, rather than run the risk of being considered outré, and doing harm to the cause.' The suffragette newspaper *Votes for Women* also commented, in 1908 that, 'The Suffragette of today is dainty and precise in her dress.'

As membership grew, supporters chose to wear a small symbol of the movement in the Suffragette colours, such as a broach on their blouse or a rosette. These tokens were available for sale in London department stores such as Selfridges and Liberty, where women could also purchase striped ribbons to

A 1913 protest by suffragettes in London.

decorate their hats, along with suffragette-themed underwear, slippers and soap.

In America, the National Woman's Party in 1917 organised a silent watch outside the White House which lasted for two years, and which attracted 2,000 women who dressed in white – one of the colours, alongside purple and gold, chosen to represent their movement. They, too, were dismissed by men and described by Republican representative Joseph Walk of Massachusetts in 1917 as 'bewildered, deluded creatures with short skirts and short hair'. Eventually the suffragette movement succeeded in their cause. Women over thirty years of age, with property, won the right to vote in Britain in 1918, and in the United States in 1919, when the Nineteenth Amendment was enacted. As a tribute to the dedication of these women, the colour white has frequently been worn by female politicians, from Shirley Chisholm after being the first black women elected into Congress in 1969, to Hilary Clinton during her presidential campaign in 2016.

THE BANANA DANCE

THE BANANA SKIRT
JOSEPHINE BAKER
1926

In October 1925 a young African-American dancer from St Louis came out onto the stage at the Théâtre des Champs-Elysées in Paris, and immediately enraptured the city. Baker had been marketed as a Harlem jazz baby and an exotic flapper, as part of the La Revue Nègre, a spectacular musical which was designed to promote Black culture. Josephine's moment on stage was called La Danse Sauvage, for which she was naked except for feathers around her waist.

At first it seemed like a step back for Baker, who had come to Paris to enhance her career as a dancer and not be treated as a novelty act. Her reception was so different from New York, where she was forbidden from entering certain department stores and nightclubs because of the colour of her skin. With the extraordinary demand for Baker, she was snapped up by music hall, the Folies Bergère, to bring her star power to their stage.

She descended from a tree branch suspended over the stage, dressed only in a tutu made up of sixteen rubber bananas, where she performed a Charleston at lightning fast speed, and used her signature moves of eye rolls and high kicks to mock the savage image the dance represented. It became known as the Banana Dance, and was a signature performance for her. The banana skirt became a symbol of the jazz age, and of how African-American performances could twist offensive racial stereotypes, manipulating them, reclaiming identity.

From that moment, Josephine Baker revolutionized the way Black people, and Black women in particular, were seen. She became extraordinarily wealthy from her performances, which drew people from all over the world. There were dolls of Baker, and her sleek hair and body were used to promote her new beauty products, while glittering skullcaps were sold to replicate her Eton crop hair. But when Sem, the cartoonist, portrayed a caricature of Josephine dressed in elegant evening dress, with a monkey tail swinging from behind, it was an offensive reminder that to many she was still considered a savage novelty.

Growing tired of playing up to racial stereotypes, by the end of 1926, she opened her own nightclub, Chez Joséphine, in the heart of Montmartre. During World War II, she worked closely with the French Resistance against the Nazis – her way of fighting against the racism she had experienced throughout her life. Through her groundbreaking dance, but also her talent and grace, Baker shook up notions of gender and race and opened the door for other Black women to reclaim their power through performance. Decades later, Beyoncé paid tribute to the celebrated icon in her 2006 Fashion Rocks performance, when she donned a banana skirt fashioned after Baker's own.

Josephine Baker in her banana skirt, 1926.

MODERNISM AND LIBERATION 1890–1930

THE POWER OF BLACK

THE LITTLE BLACK DRESS
COCO CHANEL
1926

The Little Black Dress (LBD) is the wardrobe staple that swept the world from its conception in the 1920s through to Audrey Hepburn wearing Givenchy in the iconic film *Breakfast at Tiffany's* and Elizabeth Hurley in a Versace safety-pin dress. Princess Diana famously wore her black 'revenge' dress by Christina Stambolian in June 1994, on the same night that Prince Charles' tell-all documentary on their marriage was due to air. The LBD is not only a powerful statement piece but it has become the reliable favourite, flattering to all figures, worn by all sizes and ages.

The LBD's origins lie in the concept of Coco Chanel's desire to make fashion more functional for women and was the culmination of her groundbreaking garçonne style in the 1920s. Chanel's jersey sweaters, short pleated skirts and dropped waistlines suited the new generation of active, modern women in pursuit of a more liberal lifestyle, who cut their hair short, tanned their skin and danced all night. Her simple styles could also be replicated easily, allowing for their imitation for girls on all budgets. The colour black in particular offered utilitarian simplicity; it was strong, wearable and could transition from day to night. 'For four or five years I made only black,' she said. 'My dresses sold like mad with little touches – a white collar, or cuffs. Everyone wore them – actresses, society women, housemaids.'

When Chanel's black sheath dress first appeared in American *Vogue* in October 1926, the fashion bible hailed it as the fashion equivalent of the Ford motorcar, which had been revolutionary for its mass manufacture. They wrote: 'The Chanel "Ford" – the frock that all the world will wear – is model "817" of black crêpe de Chine. The bodice blouses slightly at [the] front and sides and has a tight bolero at the back. Especially chic is the arrangement of tiny tucks which cross in front; imported by Saks Fifth Avenue.' It was called 'little' because it was discreet, and the black fabric acted as a canvas to allow women to add their own accessories, such as a string of white pearls or a flower corsage.

Chanel boldly proclaimed that 'before me no one would have dared to dress in black'. For centuries, black was considered the colour of mourning, and the Victorians in particular promoted black for widows. Women were expected to be shrouded in matte black gowns and veils for two years after the death of their husbands. Black was thought to be too dramatic to be worn in such a stark way during the day, rather than solely as an evening dress, but there were notable exceptions. In 1884, painter John Singer Sargent caused a scandal when he displayed his portrait of Madame Pierre Gautreu in a plunging black satin gown

Coco Chanel's little black dress, 1926.

MODERNISM AND LIBERATION 1890–1930

with thin straps. The dress was so revealing and the colour so bold, that Sargent changed the name of the portrait to Madame X to protect the identity of the sitter. After World War I, black not only expressed a collective grief for the millions who were killed but was also accepted as a practical and adaptable colour as more women went into the workplace.

The stark nature of Chanel's black dresses made a huge impact, but the colour wasn't novel for Chanel – she had used black in her collections since 1917 – and other designers, like Paul Poiret, had also experimented with the colour in the 1910s. But it was because of Chanel's vision that the expression the 'Little Black Dress' would enter into fashion lexicon as a byword for elegance. As Chanel once said: 'Women think of every colour, except the absence of colours. I have said that black had everything. White too. They have an absolute beauty. It is perfect harmony. Dress women in white or black at a ball: they are the only ones you see.'

'BEFORE ME NO ONE WOULD HAVE DARED TO DRESS IN BLACK,'

COCO CHANEL

Actress Louise Brooks epitomized the flapper look.

The 1920s was the decade of change, where the horrors of the Great War and the Spanish Flu pandemic sparked a drive for liberation among the population, and the flapper, the term given to a woman who behaved unconventionally, was the carefree symbol of that era. Fuelled by a booming economy, these frivolous women embraced taboos by drinking cocktails and smoking, and hitting the dance floor with inventive new moves. They wore loose chemise dresses that revealed their legs, and rather than emphasise the female body, the waist hung low and they flattened their chests to create an androgynous silhouette.

The name 'flapper' came into mainstream use around 1920 when Olive Thomas starred in the film *The Flapper*, and F. Scott Fitzgerald published his collection of short stories, *Flappers and Philosophers*. Inspired by another Hollywood star, Colleen Moore in the 1920 *Flaming Youth*, women chopped their hair into the controversially short bob hairstyle. Louise Brooks' shingle cut was one of the most copied, and women's faces also became more prominent, their eyes rimmed with heavy black kohl and lips painted into a pouting cupid's bow. The trailblazing flapper set out to shock the older generation and led the charge in how women could conduct themselves in the post-war world.

Leading the charge was writer Zelda Fitzgerald, who summed up her generation in 1922's 'Eulogy on the Flapper'. She wrote: 'She flirted because it was fun to flirt and wore a one-piece bathing suit because she had a good figure, she covered her face with powder and paint because she didn't need it and she refused to be bored chiefly because she wasn't boring.'

A GENDER-DEFYING SPECTACLE

THE TUXEDO
MARLENE DIETRICH
1930

When Marlene Dietrich wore a gentleman's tuxedo in *Morocco* in 1930, complete with top hat and bow tie, it was a shocking and powerful depiction of a woman straying from the conventions of accepted gendered fashion. By cross-dressing and kissing a woman on the lips in the film, the star was deliberately provocative and challenging the status quo.

German-born Dietrich had arrived in the US that same year, and created shock-waves among conservative Americans with her penchant for wearing trousers, both on and off screen. She'd already made a name for herself with her performance in Josef von Sternberg's *The Blue Angel* (1930), where her lean legs were fetishised, and her preference for trousers in real life was initially dismissed as a publicity stunt. In an article in *Motion Picture*, 'Marlene Dietrich Tells Why She Doesn't Wear Men's Clothes!', she commented: 'I am sincere in my preference for men's clothes – I do not wear them to be sensational ... I think I am much more alluring in these clothes.'

Von Sternberg and Dietrich were reunited in the film actress's American debut, *Morocco*, where she played cabaret singer Amy Jolly. She was inspired by the drag artists of 1920s Berlin cabaret to wear a tuxedo and, after von Sternberg saw her wearing one, complete with top hat, at a Berlin party, he decided that would be the costume for her first appearance on screen.

When it came to honing Dietrich's cabaret performances, she also took inspiration from the cross-dressing of Black blues performers. In the 1920s, during the Harlem Renaissance, a Black cultural and social movement centred around the New York district, African-American singers like Gladys Bentley and Ma Rainey signposted their lesbianism by dressing in tuxedos. Ma Bentley's 'Prove It to Me Blues' hints at her queerness with the lines, 'It's true I wear a collar and tie' and 'went out last night with a crowd of my friends; They must've been women, 'cause I don't like no men.'

While the tuxedo was designed to create a strong male silhouette, when worn by a woman it presented a sense of forbidden sexuality. By wearing androgynous clothing in the late nineteenth and early twentieth centuries, women used it both as a code to signify sexual preference and as a symbol of 'non-verbal resistance' against their expected gender roles.

In a scene in *Morocco* that echoes the real-life audience reaction, Amy Jolly's masculine appearance initially provokes boos from the cabaret audience, until she titillates them by flouting conventions of the time and kissing a woman on the lips. 'First I uncovered my legs, and people were excited over that. Now I cover my

Marlene Dietrich in *Morocco*, 1930.

legs, and that excites them, too,' said Dietrich. The innuendo about Dietrich's transgressive European sexuality was designed to turn on both male and female audiences, at a time when gender ambiguity could be shown in Hollywood films – before the strict censorship codes were introduced in 1934.

Von Sternberg later commented, 'I not only wished to touch lightly on a lesbian accent but also demonstrate that her [Dietrich's] sensual appeal was not entirely due to the classic formation of her legs. Having her wear trousers was not meant to stimulate a fashion which not long after the film was shown to encourage women to ignore skirts in favour of the less picturesque lower half of male attire.'

In the context of Depression-era America, when the increasing number of women entering the workplace were blamed for rising male unemployment, Dietrich choosing to emulate masculine style was considered deliberately confrontational. While other actresses and fashion icons like Katharine Hepburn and Greta Garbo opted for trousers and 'power suits' in their personal life, it was a style that only the most daring and privileged of women could pull off in this period. That is, until the advent of World War II when women again moved back into the workforce in droves, taking on jobs previously done by men and often necessitating the wearing of more masculine attire.

Today, many style icons have paid a nod to Dietrich's tuxedo moment, donning this strong fashion statement on the red carpet and at events like the Met Ball – Madonna, Rihanna, Diane Keaton and Angelina Jolie, among them.

'I AM SINCERE IN MY PREFERENCE FOR MEN'S CLOTHES – I DO NOT WEAR THEM TO BE SENSATIONAL ... I THINK I AM MUCH MORE ALLURING IN THESE CLOTHES.'

MARLENE DIETRICH

TAMARA DE LEMPICKA – THE MODERN WOMAN

In her portrait of the Duchess of La Salle (1925), artist Tamara de Lempicka depicts a woman very much in control of her own image. Standing in a confident pose and dressed in a man's suit and riding boots, her hair cut into a shiny Eton crop, she almost dares the viewer as she confronts them in the androgynous style that was prevalent in the 1920s.

The art deco artist was similarly striking in appearance in real life. Having escaped the Russian Revolution for Paris in 1917, she established herself in the Left Bank of the city as an openly bisexual bohemian. Her cubist works captured the glamour and sexuality of her subjects and came to represent women's liberation. She became one of the most fashionable artists of the 1920s, reflecting the acceptance of gay women during this era, before a rise of conservatism in the 1930s. Her paintings conveyed the new sense of freedom felt by independent women in the post-war period – the shining satin gowns that cling to languorous bodies, the tilt of a hat from which her subjects glance from under and the diaphanous fabrics held against naked bodies. These elegant women looked like they'd stepped out of the pages of fashion magazines.

One of de Lempicka's most famous works, her 1929 *Self-portrait (Tamara in the Green Bugatti)*, came to stand as an image of the modern woman. Commissioned for the cover of *Die Dame (The Lady)*, the German fashion magazine, the painting depicts de Lempicka as a striking, empowered woman behind the wheel of her sports car, who is absolutely in charge of her destiny.

MID-CENTURY STYLE

STYLE

1931–1953

The Wall Street Crash of 1929 marked an end to the optimism of the 1920s as it triggered a global recession. Over the next decade, the Great Depression gripped the United States and Europe. In the US, by 1932, twelve million people were unemployed and around one out of every four families no longer had an income.

To find some escapism from the headlines about mass unemployment, the long bread lines and the fears around a new world conflict as fascism took hold in Italy and Germany, fashions became more conservative, returning to a sense of Edwardian romanticism. The change in silhouette, from the knee-length flapper dresses to floor-skimming gowns, was dramatic, and was partly instigated by French couturier Madeleine Vionnet, who experimented with a bias cut to create luxurious, shimmering gowns.

1930S STYLE

In some respects the 1930s was an optimistic time as there were increased rights for workers, allowing for designated working hours and more leisure time. Towns were lit up with entertainment venues such as cinemas and dance halls, more households were able to buy radios and motorcars and new suburbs sprung up in the countryside to ease the pressures of overcrowding in cities.

Writer George Orwell in his seminal *The Road to Wigan Pier* illustrated how the magic of the movies and more accessible and cheaper clothing offered a sense of escapism to working men and women. 'You may have three halfpence in your pocket and not a prospect in the world, and only the corner of a leaky bedroom to go home to; but in your new clothes you can stand on the street corner, indulging in a private daydream of yourself as Clark Gable or Greta Garbo, which compensates you for a great deal.'

'OUR PAGES IN *VOGUE* REFLECTED A NEW AUSTERITY ... STRAIGHT UP-AND-DOWN FASHIONS WITH LITTLE FABRIC TO THEM ...'

BETTINA BALLARD

Ready-to-wear fashion was a new concept that first emerged in the US in the 1920s on New York's Seventh Avenue, with manufacturers creating more accessible clothing based on the high-end couture coming out of Paris. Hattie Carnegie was a pioneer in creating chic but more affordable clothing, when she launched her ready-to-wear fashion line in 1928. Claire McCardell took it further by redefining utility-wear for women with her innovative clothing that was multi-functional, such as her pop-over dress.

NEW YORK VS PARIS

The outbreak of World War II in Europe in 1939, and the occupation of Paris in 1940, had a dramatic impact on fashion, from the rationing of clothing put in place to the ubiquity of uniforms, as worn by the millions of men and women around the world who signed up to the armed forces. With Parisian designers unable to lead on fashion in the ways they had in the previous two decades, American designers aimed to make New York City fashion capital of the world. This helped shape a more functional style of dress that suited the relaxed, egalitarian lifestyle in the United States.

Following the end of the war in 1945, Parisian couturiers sought to reclaim their place as fashion instigators. Christian Dior launched his New Look, which heralded a return to the feminine silhouette, and groundbreaking designers like Cristóbel Balenciaga experimented with radical shapes and cut.

1930

→ Marlene Dietrich makes her American film debut in *Morocco*, performing in a tuxedo.

1932

→ Joan Crawford stars in *Letty Lynton*, wearing a spectacular creation by Adrian, which inspired thousands of copies.

1936

→ Diana Vreeland is appointed as fashion editor for *Harper's Bazaar*.

1937

→ Elsa Schiaparelli teams up with surrealist designer Salvador Dalí on a number of collaborations, including the lobster-print dress.
→ Cristóbal Balenciaga opens his Paris couture house on Avenue George V.

1939

→ Britain and France declare war on Germany, following the latter's invasion of Poland, marking the start of World War II.
→ Madeleine Vionnet retires and, on the outbreak of war, Coco Chanel closes her fashion house.
→ Horst P. Horst photographs the elegant corset featured in Mainbocher's last Parisian collection.
→ Greta Garbo stars in *Ninotchka*, wearing a funnel hat by Adrian, which was inspired by the surrealist collaboration between Schiaparelli and Dalí.

1940

→ France is occupied by Germany, leading to restrictions on fashions coming out of Paris.

1941

→ In June, clothes rationing is introduced in Britain.
→ The United States enters the war following Japan's attack on Pearl Harbor.

1942

→ Ready-to-wear designer Claire McCardell introduces her Pop-over dress.
→ Fabric rationing is introduced in the United States.
→ The British government launch their utility clothing scheme, encouraging designers to manufacture wardrobe essentials to be sold on the high street.

1943
→ Cab Calloway stars in the African-American musical *Stormy Weather* (1943) wearing a zoot suit.
→ Reports of riots breaking out in US cities between US servicemen and Latino teenagers dressed in zoot suits.

1944
→ Following the liberation of Paris by the Allies, French women are noted for their use of patriotic fashion to resist and rebel.

1945
→ Victory in Europe and Japan mark the end of World War II.

1946
→ Christian Dior opens his fashion house in Paris.
→ Louis Réard invents the daring two-piece swimsuit, which he names the 'bikini', after the first post-war nuclear testing at Bikini Atoll.

1947
→ Christian Dior launches his revolutionary New Look, which enhances the feminine silhouette.

1949
→ Clothing rationing in Britain comes to an end.

1952
→ Hubert de Givenchy opens his first salon in Paris and Audrey Hepburn becomes one of his first celebrity clients.

1953
→ Queen Elizabeth II crowned queen of England.
→ Cristóbal Balenciaga launches his balloon jacket, reinventing the way clothing enhances a woman's body.

ABSTRACT BEAUTY

LOBSTER DRESS
ELSA SCHIAPARELLI AND SALVADOR DALÍ
1937

In 1937, when Italian designer Elsa Schiaparelli displayed a white dinner dress with a bold print of a lobster, it perfectly demonstrated the merging of fashion and art. The lobster design was a favourite motif of her friend Salvador Dalí, who had featured it in his works from 1934, including *New York Dream – Man Finds Lobster in Place of Phone,* which he brought to life for his lobster telephone sculpture in 1936. Dalí drew the initial motif for the Lobster dress, and Schiaparelli then commissioned silk designer Sache to print it onto a white silk organza dress, which featured a bright red belt.

The Spanish artist often linked food with sex. The lobster and the position of the creature on the skirt, with the tail over the sexual organs of the wearer, added to the erotic charge of the dress. While he had wanted to add a touch of mayonnaise to his design, Schiaparelli considered it a step too far, and instead they settled for sprigs of parsley, offering the clue that the lobster and the wearer are to be the main course.

Both Dalí and Schiaparelli enjoyed pushing boundaries in their creations. Schiaparelli first made a name for herself with her popular trompe l'oeil sweaters emblazoned with a white butterfly bow. She loved designs which, in her words, 'shocked the bourgeois'; her clothes included a skeleton sweater and a swimsuit with wriggling fish on the stomach. She and Dalí collaborated, in the 1930s, on a number of surrealist, tongue-in-cheek designs, including a hat that looked like a lamb chop and a shoe with a shocking pink heel.

Schiaparelli's Lobster dress had further notoriety after Wallis Simpson chose it as part of her trousseau for her cause célèbre marriage to Edward, Duke of Windsor. Just before the wedding, Cecil Beaton photographed her wearing the dress in the gardens of the Château de Condé, and the images were splashed across an eight-page feature in *Vogue* in May 1937. Simpson was a polarizing figure, blamed for Edward choosing to abdicate from the British throne, and the dress, with its shocking, powerful and suggestive imagery, further cemented her, in some minds, as a brazen, immoral woman.

Wallis Simpson photographed by Cecil Beaton for *Vogue*, 1937.

SURREALISM IN FASHION

In the 1939 film *Ninotchka*, Greta Garbo plays a dour Russian woman who is lured into embracing capitalism after seeing a series of surrealist hats in the window of a shop on a visit to Paris. The costume designer for the film, Adrian, was influenced by Italian fashion designer Elsa Schiaparelli's collaboration with surrealist artist Salvador Dalí in creating the hats, and as Ninotchka secretly buys and wears one that looks like a funnel, it came to represent the concept of free choice and expression in comparison to the uniformity of communism.

Surrealism was an avant-garde movement that emerged in the 1920s. It fused art with philosophy and the unconscious, exploring the boundaries of reality and imagination. It derived from the theories of Karl Marx and new interest in Sigmund Freud's psychoanalysis, which tapped into dreams. Dalí, the movement's de facto leader, commented on this, in 1940: 'I try to create fantastic things, magical things, things like in a dream. The world needs more fantasy.'

By the 1930s, surrealism had moved into fashion design. Elsa Schiaparelli launched her career with her trompe l'oeil knitted sweaters with the image of a collar bow, following the surrealist concept of challenging perceptions through creating visual optics with new techniques. In 1936, she created black gloves with red tips, giving the appearance of fingernails, and a black skeleton suit with padding to create the illusion of ribs and spine on the body, taking the inside of the body outside.

Schiaparelli teamed up with Dalí in a series of collaborations, including the Lobster dress (see pages 44–45), and a Shoe Hat, where a shocking pink heel gives the impression of an upside-down stiletto on the wearer's head.

While the movement didn't cross over into her functional designs, Coco Chanel surrounded herself with surrealists, collaborating with Jean Cocteau to design costumes for his ballets and plays, and developing a friendship with Dalí. He stayed at Chanel's French Riviera villa, where it's believed he created a number of important works, including

The black felt Shoe Hat by
Schiaparelli and Dali, 1937.

Apparition of Face and Fruit Dish on a Beach (1938).
The two also worked together to design surrealist
costumes for Stravinsky's *Bacchanale* ballet in 1939,
which featured some of Dalí's best-known signatures,
a hoop dress with teeth and lobster motifs.

Dalí frequently appeared in *Vogue* in the 1930s,
further cementing his surrealist vision with the world
of fashion, through his illustrations, articles and cover
designs. Leading fashion photographer Horst P. Horst
also borrowed from surrealism in his portraits
focusing on particular body parts, such as his 1941
image of linked hands, his focus on bare feet, and of
the bare back in, arguably his most famous work, the
1939 *Mainbocher Corset* (see pages 48–49).

MID-CENTURY STYLE 1931–1953

BEAUTY BY DESIGN

MAINBOCHER CORSET
PHOTOGRAPHED BY HORST P. HORST
1939

One of the most striking compositions in fashion photography, Horst P. Horst's image of a luxurious corset by the Parisian designer Mainbocher dropped a bombshell when it was published in *Vogue* in 1939.

Using his skills in architecture and still-life photography, Horst's image has an erotic charge in the sculptural properties of the model's back, contrasted with the intricate structure of the corset and the flow of the ribbons. Taken in *Vogue*'s Parisian studio in August 1939, Horst carefully prepared the lighting in advance to capture the highlights and deep shadows of her back, creating an unusual image in its celebration of the musculature of a woman's body.

Born Horst Paul Albert Bohrmann in Germany in 1906, he moved to Paris as a young man to work as assistant to the revered architect Le Corbusier. After becoming close friends with French *Vogue*'s photographer George Hoyningen-Huene, he was introduced to the magazine's art director, which led to him being commissioned as one of their photographers in 1931. He later recalled how he 'knew nothing about fashion, so I just learned as I went along, used my minor architectural training as a rough guide, and tried to create a sense of elegance for myself'.

The 1930s was the age of fashion photography, when new artists like Horst experimented with their craft. He was a classicist in his influences, and his aesthetics referenced the geometry of art deco and the avant-garde of surrealism, using carefully planned lighting and composition to dramatic effect. He also photographed some of the most notable people of the era, including Coco Chanel, Bette Davis and Marlene Dietrich, whom he imbued with an other-worldly glamour and sophistication.

Horst liked to capture women as Greek goddesses, 'almost unattainable, slightly statuesque, and in Olympian peace'. He often used props to link his images to the classical world, as per his architectural training under Le Corbusier; and in his Mainbocher corset photograph, the semi-nude body seems to flow from the marble balustrade.

Such was the impact of the image that, when it was published in *Vogue*, with a little retouching to create a waspish waist, it evoked fresh excitement for the corset as an elaborate and beautiful undergarment, with the corseted shape becoming an important feature of the fashion shows of 1939. American *Vogue* announced that the corset was 'the key to new Paris silhouettes'. However, the luxury and extravagance of these fashions would be delayed by the outbreak of World War II in Europe.

Madame Bernon modelling Mainbocher's corset in Horst's famous image.

The photo would be the last Horst would take in Paris before the war. Straight after shooting the image, in August 1939, Horst fled France by boarding the SS *Normandie* for the United States, on its last transatlantic voyage in peacetime. He established himself in America, successfully applied for citizenship in 1943, then signed up to the army as a war photographer, but he always looked back with sadness at having to leave France. 'I had found a family in Paris, and a way of life. The clothes, the books, the apartment, everything was left behind … This photograph [*Mainbocher Corset*] is peculiar – for me it is the essence of that moment. While I was taking it, I was thinking of all that I was leaving behind.'

Mainbocher also moved from Paris to the United States with the outbreak of World War II and his focus shifted. Instead of further developing his line of corsets, he was commissioned to design a uniform for the women's US Navy Corps. The photo, with all its beauty and excess, was a reminder, as journalist Janet Flanner observed, that 'the thirties were over'.

Fifty years later, Horst's photo became well known to a new generation of people when Madonna recreated the image as one of her inspirations for her 1990 music video for 'Vogue', which served as her homage to mid-century glamour. While she saw it as a tribute to his work, Horst wasn't so enamoured, believing he should have been recompensed for the use of his ideas.

'WE NEVER THOUGHT OF IT AS FASHION WHEN I WAS IN PARIS … IT WAS L'ELEGANCE, THE WAY WE LIVED.'

HORST P. HORST

When Britain declared war on Germany on 3 September 1939, a wave of khaki and blue serge swept across the country as men and women enlisted in the armed forces. The outbreak of World War II had an immediate impact on fashion, and not just through the uniforms that every young man and woman was expected to wear. With blockades preventing imports into Britain, and with an immediate demand for wool for uniforms, textile rationing was introduced in June 1941, severely limiting the amount of new clothing people could buy.

While the 1930s had been defined by romanticised fashion and floor-length gowns, women's dress followed a military style with knee-length skirts, jackets and blouses. The British government encouraged designers to take part in their utility clothing scheme in 1942, to mass-manufacture wardrobe essentials for sale on the high street. Rationing also sparked a new sense of creativity in 'Make Do and Mend', as women recycled and adapted their clothing, personalised their gas mask cases and pencilled seams onto their legs to mimic hard-to-find silk stockings.

The United States joined the war in December 1941, following the Japanese attack on Pearl Harbor, and when it was realised that American women would be required for war work, fashion magazines became champions of women in uniform, with *Vogue* naming them as their 'Best Dressed Women in the World Today' in 1943. As *Vogue* fashion editor Bettina Ballard recalled, 'our pages in *Vogue* reflected a new austerity ... straight up-and-down fashions with little fabric to them the smart patriotic thing to wear'.

UTILITY CHIC

POP-OVER DRESS
CLAIRE MCCARDELL
1942

When *Harper's Bazaar* offered a challenge to designers to create a dress that could transition from housework to cocktail party, Claire McCardell's Pop-over dress was the answer – and proved to be an overwhelming success when she launched it in 1942.

Maryland-born McCardell began her career in 1930 as an assistant to Robert Turk at the mass-manufacturing firm Townley Frocks. Following Turk's accidental death, McCardell was asked to finish his collections, and from there she became the most recognisable designer at Townley.

McCardell looked to street fashion for her inspiration, and she specialised in versatile designs that could be affordable for every woman. As a busy New York woman, she lamented the 'crinolines' that 'got stuck in revolving doors', and took inspiration from the pockets of men's clothing because 'men are free from the clothes problem – why should I not follow their example?' McCardell's 1938 Monastic dress was her first big hit. Tent-like in structure, it came with a versatile belt to adapt to a woman's body; it was copied widely.

With America entering the war in December 1941, there was a desire for utility-wear and adaptable dresses, particularly after fabric rationing was introduced. The Pop-over was a simple grey wrap dress, which featured a deep pocket for practicality, and which could be used as a beach wrap, as a house dress for cleaning and cooking and then transition into the evening. A publicity photo by Louise Dahl-Wolfe depicted a model wearing the Pop-over, with one hand in an oven mitt and the other in the pocket, demonstrating how a woman could be both chic and house-proud.

Such was its appeal to American women, particularly with its low price of $6.95, that over 75,000 were sold by Townley in its first year of production. It became an important feature in McCardell's collection, adapted in different fabrics, such as denim and gingham. One advert for the Pop-over described it as 'the original utility fashion', 'equally at home in the kitchen, at play or outdoors'.

The dress was acclaimed by the American Fashion Critics Association and, by the 1950s, McCardell was a star designer. Her clothes spoke for the confident, relaxed and athletic American woman. And while she might not have had the pizzazz of contemporaries like Christian Dior, McCardell was groundbreaking in her versatility, which tapped into a more egalitarian mid-twentieth-century style.

Diana Vreeland, later a champion of McCardell, once described one of her dresses as 'pathetic', but it was precisely their difference from the dominant structured silhouettes of the time that made McCardell's designs so refreshing.

The Pop-over dress, as featured in a Montgomery Ward catalogue in 1943.

HOLLYWOOD FASHION

America was in the midst of the Great Depression in the early 1930s, with millions out of work and struggling to find food. But in Hollywood, the movie industry was booming. The costume designers at the major studios worked hard to create the awe-inspiring creations for their glamorous stars, which were proving to be so popular with audiences.

Each week, eighty-five million Americans queued outside movie theatres to experience the mysterious beauty of Greta Garbo, the synchronised chorus lines of Busby Berkeley musicals, Fred Astaire and Ginger Rogers on the dance floor and glamour girls, like Carole Lombard and Jean Harlow, sipping champagne and slinking in satin gowns at society parties.

Almost as soon as the Wall Street stock market crashed, hems dropped to the floor and waists were raised to their natural placing. Femininity was highlighted in bias-cut, figure-hugging gowns in luxurious fabrics, creating a sense of escapism. The white satin gown was a staple of 1930s cinema, which shimmered in the black-and-white film.

Travis Banton was the favourite designer of Marlene Dietrich, working with her and director Josef von Sternberg to create a classic image of masculine tailoring. MGM's star designer Adrian transformed the wardrobe department into a bustling clothing factory as he set trends across the United States. He created Joan Crawford's broad-shouldered silhouette, glittering skullcaps for Greta Garbo and bias-cut satin gowns for Jean Harlow. His designs, much to his annoyance, were constantly copied and displayed in department stores like Macy's and Sears. A version of a heavily ruffled, white organdie gown, worn by Joan Crawford in *Letty Lynton*, sold a reported 500,000 copies in Macy's. Adrian helped to make fashion accessible to every woman who watched her favourite actress in a darkened movie theatre and lusted after her clothes.

As Hollywood became the new fashion capital, movies were promoted for their costumes, with pictures sent out to the press of stars in the latest designs. *Photoplay* magazine, in 1931, introduced a

Joan Crawford in the puffed sleeve *Letty Lynton* dress designed by Adrian, 1932.

Hollywood Fashions spread, which advertised its own clothing label based on the styles of stars. As *Silver Screen* magazine wrote, in 1932: 'Paris may decree this and Paris may decree that, but when that Crawford girl pops up in puffed sleeves, then it's puffed sleeves for us before tea-time.'

After the outbreak of World War II, the studios continued to reflect societal changes, even as they were hit by fabric rationing. They followed the trend for austerity with simpler silhouettes and military-inspired tailoring. While costume designers like Edith Head continued to create showstopping gowns in the post-war 1950s, they would never yield as much power over the fashion industry as they had done in the Golden Age of the 1930s.

AUDACIOUS STREET STYLE

THE ZOOT SUIT
CAB CALLOWAY
1943

The zoot suit was a fashion statement which emerged in urban Black and Hispanic communities in the late 1930s as an audacious way to stand out. Heavily influenced by jazz singer Cab Calloway, who wore a range of zoot suits for his stage performances and in the hit film *Stormy Weather* (1943), the zoot suit was a proud statement of emerging African-American cultural identity, as the young men who wore them refused to be subservient.

'Zoot' meant an exaggerated and extravagant style, and these suits were all about making a dramatic impression – large, padded shoulders, a long drape with wide lapels and high-waisted trousers that flared at the knee and tapered in at the ankle. They were topped with a wide-brimmed hat, ducktail hairstyle, thick-soled pointed shoes and a long watch chain.

It was a style worn by Detroit Red, the young hustler who would become Malcolm X. In his autobiography, he recalled the excitement of purchasing his first zoot suit at the age of fifteen.

He said: 'I took three of those twenty-five-cent, sepia-toned, while-you-wait pictures of myself, posed the way 'hipsters' wearing their zoots would 'cool it' – hat angled, knees drawn close together, feet wide apart, both index fingers jabbed toward the floor. The long coat and swinging chain and the Punjab pants were much more dramatic if you stood that way.'

It would also be adopted by young Mexican-Americans, where it became known as 'pachuco' style. They were the children of immigrants who had moved to the cities to seek work following a lack of rural jobs during the Depression, and their way of rebelling was through wearing the zoot suit. A 1942 *Newsweek* story reported the pachucos in vivid, garish suits, with polka-dot shirts, 'string ties, pearl buttons as big as silver dollars, and trousers so tight they have to be zipped'.

When the War Production Board put in place texture rationing, the zoot suit, with its profuse use of fabric, became a marker of defiance. Cab Calloway's *Stormy Weather* suit, said to have cost $185, and using an excessive amount of fabric, was made before rationed orders were introduced.

'Jitterbug dancers and the strange, voluminous garb that many of them affect are interfering with the progress of the country's war effort and the War Production Board intends to do something about it,' wrote *The New York Times* in 1942. 'It is wasting a large amount of fabric that ought to be saved for our soldiers and for necessary civilian clothing.'

The self-assertiveness of zoot suiters, combined with a disregard for rationing at a time of war, exasperated white America. World War II brought

Cab Calloway in the 1943 film *Stormy Weather*.

MID-CENTURY STYLE 1931–1953

simmering racial tensions to the surface, despite whites and non-whites serving side by side in battle. Yet as young white military recruits prepared to be shipped to fight overseas, they released the pressure by drinking and roaming the streets in their down time, where they were triggered by the young zoot-suiters in their ration-defying civilian clothing.

This culture clash culminated in the June 1943 Zoot Suit riots in Los Angeles, where servicemen entered Black and Hispanic neighbourhoods, dragging zoot-suiters from streetcars, cinema and buses, ripping off their clothes and burning them and cutting off their ducktail hair. The press and police were more sympathetic to the servicemen than the generally non-white zoot-suiters, who were stripped, beaten and humiliated. The local authorities banned the zoot suit and closed down areas to servicemen, but riots spread to other cities including Philadelphia, Detroit and Montreal.

After the war ended in 1945, and rationing was relaxed, the zoot suit became more mainstream. By 1948, a slimmer version was marketed to white Americans as a 'bold look' and was adopted by white jazz aficionados like Bing Crosby, who would take on elements of what was originally seen as Black fashion.

As Shane and Graham White explore in the book *Stylin'*, African-American men and women, when they had space to do so, 'often fashioned for themselves a distinctive and visually arresting appearance'. The zoot suit defied the theory of emulation, as the fashion began with low-status groups of Mexican-American and African-American youth, and rose up to influence mainstream white male dress; a phenomenon evident in other movements, such as hip-hop.

'YOU GOT TO BE TRICKING YOURSELF OUT LIKE THE DUDE, GET YOURSELF UP IN SOME PANTS WITH STUFF-CUFFS, REET-PLEATS, LOOK LIKE A ZOOT, WALK LIKE A ZOOT, TALK LIKE A ZOOT.'

THOMAS SANCHEZ

The popularity of dance moves like the turkey trot, the shimmy and the black bottom in the 1920s helped shape a new fashion for freedom-giving clothing on dance floors in Britain and America, but their influence originated in the Black communities of Harlem and New Orleans, throbbing with the sounds of ragtime, jazz and the blues.

New York's district of Harlem was a self-enclosed world of Black-owned businesses, entertainment and political and social life, formed from a mass immigration of Black people from the Southern states after the end of the Civil War. By the 1920s, the Harlem Renaissance was in its heyday, centred in the New York district and focusing on African-American arts and culture. Prominent figures included writer Langston Hughes, singers Josephine Baker, Gladys Bentley and Ma Rainey, and CJ Walker, the first female, self-made millionaire in America with her line of beauty products for Black women.

Some of the greatest jazz musicians worked in Harlem in the 1920s, with clubs and bars on every corner playing blues and jazz. Actress and writer Anita Loos called it 'the gayest place that America ever produced'. Musicians like Louis Armstrong and Duke Ellington were celebrated by white audiences, and there was a flourishing lesbian and gay culture, reflected in blues musicians like Bessie Smith and Lucille Bogan. As Harlem Renaissance writer Langston Hughes once said, 'it was the period when negroes were in vogue'.

Black people created their own style, which would then be appropriated by white culture, from the sound of hot jazz and the 'hep cat' style of the zoot suit, to rock 'n' roll and jazz and bebop musicians Miles Davis and Charlie Parker, whose sharp Brooks Brothers tailoring was emulated in Ivy League and mod fashions.

THE BEACHWEAR BOMBSHELL

THE BIKINI
LOUIS RÉARD
1946

When the United States carried out the first post-war nuclear weapon testing at Bikini Atoll in 1946, it not only caused reverberations in the South Pacific, but its name would lend itself to a skimpy new garment that caused shockwaves around the world.

While two-piece bathing suits became increasingly popular during World War II as a result of fabric rationing, in May 1946 French designer Jacques Heim created what is considered the first modern incarnation of the bikini, which revealed more skin than ever before. He named it 'Atome', to capture the headline-generating excitement of the nuclear tests and billed it as 'the world's smallest bathing suit', which he sold from his Cannes boutique in the South of France.

Heim's design was quickly followed by French engineer Louis Réard, who had taken over his mother's lingerie business in 1940. He was inspired to reinvent the swimsuit when he noticed women on the beach in St Tropez rolling up their bathing suits to improve their tan. He introduced an even skimpier swimsuit which he called the 'bikini', consisting of four triangles of fabric, only 30 inches in total, which were held together with string. It debuted in Paris on 5 July 1946, worn by 19-year-old dancer Micheline Bernardini, who agreed to wear it only when the other models refused to display themselves in such a revealing piece of clothing.

In 1947, a green-and-white, polka-dot bikini by US designer Carolyn Schnurer featured in the American edition of *Harper's Bazaar*, and immediately caused outrage, particularly with its exposure of the belly button, a part of the body considered especially risqué.

It was actress Brigitte Bardot who sparked the craze for bikinis and helped to define the French Riviera beach babe. When she made an appearance at the Cannes Film Festival in 1953, posing on the shoreline in a floral two-piece, she was mobbed by paparazzi and the image of her bikini-clad body was splashed on newpaper covers around the world. Despite the influence of Bardot, women on some beaches on France's Atlantic coast and throughout Italy were issued fines for wearing the two-piece swimsuit.

In the United States, the bikini was dismissed as a French whim, and was considered inappropriate to wear on the beach, as it went against the 1950s push for conservative family values. It was only acceptable for Hollywood starlets in 'cheesecake' photos or in the popular B-movie beach movies.

Pat Hall modeling the bikini, 1950.

The most prevalent swimwear of that era was the structured swimsuit, which embodied the feminine silhouette standardised by Christian Dior's New Look. As *Life* magazine commented in May 1950: 'American women ... have long ago rejected France's famous beachwear innovation, the scanty, two-piece Bikini bathing suit.'

There were even reports of women being fined or summoned to court for wearing bikinis on American beaches. It took almost fifteen years from its conception for the bikini to be finally accepted as suitable beachwear. *The New York Times*, in February 1959, reported that the bikini 'has exploded into the news' and 'suddenly crashed Fifth Avenue shops after a prolonged snub by Americans and quoted *Harper's Bazaar* editor Diana Vreeland as professing that the 'Bikini says to me that the best things in life are free'.

The freedom to wear a bikini on the beach coincided with the emancipation of women and a demand for equality in the 1960s. It was also given a further push into the mainstream in 1962 when actress Ursula Andress lit up cinema screens when she emerged from the sea wearing a white bikini with a knife belt in the first James Bond film, *Dr No*.

While we may perceive that women have won the right to choose what they wear on the beach, in recent years there has been similar controversy over the burkini – a full-body swimsuit worn by some Muslim women. A number of towns across France in banned them from beaches in 2016, demonstrating that the choices women make for swimwear, whether they are too skimpy or cover up too much, can become a battleground between morality and civic freedom, which is often dictated by men.

'THE BIKINI SAYS TO ME THAT THE BEST THINGS IN LIFE ARE FREE,'

DIANA VREELAND

Women in Paris in 1944, wearing elaborate turbans.

Turbans may have been a fashionable accessory for women throughout the 1930s, but during World War II in Paris, they took on a whole new meaning for women under Nazi occupation. Rather than the sense of duty British and American women felt in following the rules of rationing, women in France, suffering under the occupation, used fashion as a silent form of protest.

Three months into the occupation, in 1940, the country had been stripped of its resources, including food, leather goods and fabrics, as everything of value was sent to the German Front. Rather than give in, French women believed, as *Vogue* magazine had instructed British women, that 'their duty is in beauty'.

The turban was practical for helping women keep their hair back when working, but it also allowed a colourful expression of style with limited means, when clothing during the war was hard to source. Turbans could be made out of scraps of fabric, or other salvaged materials, such as cork, cardboard or feathers.

Vogue photographer and surrealist Lee Miller was one of the first war reporters to arrive in liberated Paris. She was struck by the beautiful girls, thin and starved by war, yet riding bicycles and steeling kisses from GIs. 'Their silhouette was very queer and fascinating to me after utility and austerity England,' she remarked. Giving up fashion would have been unpatriotic – it would have been surrendering, and their way of dressing, or creating colourful turbans, was a message of resistance.

A NEW LOOK FOR A NEW ERA

THE NEW LOOK
CHRISTIAN DIOR
1947

From the moment he showed his debut spring–summer 1947 collection, Christian Dior shook up fashion by celebrating the female silhouette after years of military uniforms and introducing what would be the pervading fashion for the next decade, the New Look.

Huge crowds gathered outside his first show on 12 February 1947, where, according to British socialite and writer Nancy Mitford, even taxi drivers were discussing Dior. During Paris's occupation by Germany in the war, women had taken to wearing defiant boxy jackets, stacked shoes and huge hats and turbans, and Dior's glamorous and luxurious style marked Paris's return as the centre of fashion. The pinnacle of Dior's first collection was the Bar suit, which featured a tailored jacket with an elegant, notched collar, worn with a pleated, ballet-length skirt.

On viewing the designer's Paris showing, Carmel Snow, the editor of US *Harper's Bazaar*, proclaimed it a 'revolution' and 'such a new look', because it was the antithesis of textile rationing and the utilitarian silhouette of the war years. Dior's gowns and suits used swathes of luxury fabric, and were inspired by the open petals of roses, lending his collection the name Corolle.

While the style was radical in shifting from the tailored, uniform-inspired clothes of the early 1940s, Dior's New Look was in essence more conservative and regressive, as it harked back to the nineteenth-century crinoline silhouette, with its use of padding, around the bust and hip, and whalebone and wire to cinch the waist. Skirts were worn over stiffened petticoats and fell almost to the ankle. At a time when there was still rationing in the UK, the New Look was denounced by British MP Mabel Ridealgh as being 'a stupidly exaggerated use of material'. Coco Chanel was also critical of this new restrictive dress. 'Dior doesn't dress women, he upholsters them,' she said.

Despite the criticism, women loved the luxury of the New Look. It was transformative in offering fairytale glamour, and when Elizabeth Taylor wore a Dior-inspired gown in *A Place in the Sun* (1951), designed by Edith Head, it became one of the most popular prom dresses for girls in America that year. Dior's vision not only marked the end of austerity but heralded a new prosperity, and a new conservatism, for the post-war years. When Dior died suddenly in 1957, it seemed to bring to an end to the New Look, as youthful rebellion would become the next force of nature in fashion.

Christian Dior's New Look, 1950.

ABSTRACT BEAUTY

THE BALLOON JACKET
CRISTÓBAL BALENCIAGA
1953

Cristóbal Balenciaga was a pioneer of modern fashion because he created signature silhouettes that defied expectations. His balloon dress and jacket were the antithesis to Christian Dior's New Look, as rather than enhancing the feminine silhouette, he encased the body in fluid fabrics to completely alter a woman's shape.

Born in the Basque region of Spain in 1895, Balenciaga began his fashion business with a small atelier in San Sebastian, Spain, before moving to the fashion capital, Paris, to open his couture house in 1937. Rather than focusing on trends, he was innovative in his cutting techniques, and like an architect explored ways to manipulate shape and fabric. He was an expert in the craft of pattern drafting to cutting, and he always began the process with the fabric, as for him, 'it's the fabric that decides'. While World War II was raging in Europe, clients risked travel to pick up his designs, particularly the 'square coat', where the sleeve was cut in one piece with the yoke.

In 1953, he introduced a silhouette that had never been seen before in women's fashion, and which was completely counterintuitive to how a woman's body was supposed to be enhanced. The balloon jacket featured a wide shape with full sleeves and a voluminous body, and rather than focusing on the waist and bust, he drew attention to the shoulders. It became a signature look, along with his balloon hem, adapted for evening gowns that were carefully constructed with boning, hoops and weights to ensure they fell in the right way. In 1957 he introduced a balloon skirt, with a single or double pouf, and his sack dress in 1958 was also radical in the way it completely eradicated the waist.

'Cristóbal Balenciaga was very unique for his time in that he was so modern-looking and avant-garde in his vision,' said Cassie Davies-Strodder, curator of the exhibition, Balenciaga: Shaping Fashion. 'Occasionally this made him unpopular, particularly with the press, whom he always liked to keep at arm's length. He only gave one newspaper interview in his entire life.'

Balenciaga was a provocateur in the way he rejected the popular hourglass shape in favour of an abstract silhouette, which was exquisitely constructed to offer a different form of beauty. Diana Vreeland, editor of American *Vogue*, called him 'the prophet of nearly every major chance in silhouette in 20 years'.

Balenciaga balloon dress, 1961, Chicago History Museum.

THE RISE OF THE COUNTER-CULTURE

1954–1984

As World War II came to a close, the next generation of young people wished to distinguish themselves from those who came before, and began to rebel against society by dressing in a unique style. The period of optimism that followed the austerity and depression of the war was marked by a rise of ever-inventive subcultures, fuelled by accessible, innovative fashions and the latest hit records that could be played on record players or listened to on jukeboxes in cafés.

The concept of the 'teenager' first emerged in the late 1930s, as swing music and hot jazz emerged from New York's Harlem to become a phenomenal source of inspiration to young people around the world. 'Hep-Jills' or 'bobbysoxers' was a term for young women mad for swing and lindy hop, who wore flat shoes, white bobby socks and short, pleated dresses that flared when they danced to the latest hits by the Benny Goodman orchestra. African-American and Latino men in urban communities also expressed their own sense of style by wearing extravagant zoot suits as a statement that they refused to adhere to mainstream society and be subservient because of their colour.

But it was in the 1950s that the teenager became a driving force, when they were identified by advertisers as a lucrative demographic to sell products to, in new ways. The teenager summed up both consumerism and individuality – rather than dressing like their parents, they made the decisions as to what they wanted to buy and wear. A 'preppy' style emerged on college campuses, later known as the Ivy League style; a rebellious counterpoint was the rock 'n' roll fashion of black leather and jeans, as popularised by Marlon Brando and James Dean. Subversive fashion

'IT WAS HIP,
IT WAS FASHIONABLE,
IT WAS CLEAN,
IT WAS GROOVY ...'

PETE TOWNSHEND

was a way to provoke and push against the norms of society and the conservative family values that were being promoted throughout the 1950s.

Later in that decade, the emerging mod subculture, initially inspired by jazz legends like Charlie Parker and Miles Davis, would filter upwards and seep into mainstream fashions and were readily available in the new boutiques (see pages 82–83) that were springing up in London's King's Road and Carnaby Street – epicentres of the Swinging London movement.

By the mid-1960s it was young people who were challenging their governments, particularly in the United States, where the hippie movement encouraged them to 'turn on, tune in, drop out' and to protest against nuclear arms and for civil and equal rights for women and minorities. This counterculture reached its peak in 1967, considered the 'Summer of Love', which saw civil unrest with protests against the Vietnam War and racial inequality. Psychedelia was introduced into fashion via Emilio Pucci's swirling-patterned dresses and kaftans in acid-hued colours and the flower prints of designer couple Ossie Clark and Celia Birtwell.

Gay pride, civil rights and women's liberation also led the way for an increase in subcultures throughout the 1970s, including the rise of hip-hop and disco, which collided together in New York. Punk reflected a sense of disaffection in Britain, at a time of strikes and unemployment, and flamboyant DIY subcultures like New Romantics and goths would be instrumental in shaping the flamboyance for the excesses of the 1980s.

1954
→ *Life* magazine in January hailed the popularity of the Ivy League Look on college campuses.
→ Levi's jeans introduce a fly zipper to their classic jeans.

1955
→ James Dean posthumously stars in *Rebel without a Cause*, dressed in Lee 101z Rider jeans.
→ Mary Quant opens the first fashion boutique, Bazaar, with Alexander Plunket Greene, on London's King's Road.

1958
→ The term 'beatnik' is coined by the press to describe the Beat Generation movement.

1961
→ John F. Kennedy becomes President of the United States.
→ André Courrèges, designer at Balenciaga, opens his own Parisian label.

1964
→ Barbara Hulanicki opens the first Biba boutique on Abingdon Road, Kensington.
→ André Courrèges launches his Space Age collection featuring his Moon Girl look.

1965
→ The escalation of US involvement in the Vietnam War.

1966
→ Paco Rabanne showcases his innovative ready-to-wear sheaths constructed from plastic and metal discs.

1967
→ Yves Saint Laurent launches his Le Smoking tuxedo.
→ The year of the Summer of Love, as hippies hold love-ins and gather at mass outdoor music festivals.
→ Emilio Pucci introduces his psychedelic-print kaftan, inspired by the hippie movement.
→ The United States makes history when the first men land on the moon.

1972

→ David Bowie releases his film *Ziggy Stardust and the Spiders from Mars*, introducing his first alter ego.

1973

→ The Biba store opens in the Derry & Toms building in Kensington.
→ The Paris fashion show known as the Battle of Versailles elevates American designers including Halston and Oscar de la Renta.

1974

→ Model Beverly Johnson becomes the first woman of colour to appear on the cover of American *Vogue*.

1975

→ The punk band the Sex Pistols are founded by Malcolm McLaren and Vivienne Westwood.

1977

→ Studio 54 opens in New York.

1979

→ The Blitz Club in Covent Garden opens, sparking the New Romantic phenomenon.
→ Margaret Thatcher is elected as British Prime Minister.

1981

→ Vivienne Westwood and Malcolm McLaren's Pirate collection is their first catwalk show.

1982

→ The Batcave, the nightclub considered the birthplace of the British goth movement, opens on London's Dean Street in Soho.

1984

→ Katharine Hamnett uses a slogan T-shirt to protest at a 10 Downing Street reception.
→ Thierry Mugler celebrates ten years as a designer in spectacular style by staging the first commercial fashion show.

IVY LEAGUE STYLE

The Ivy Look – a casual, sporty style that referenced the British aristocratic aesthetic with a functional American twist – fully came into its own on college campuses in the years following World War II.

Shaped by British dandy style at Oxford and Cambridge universities in the 1920s, it was defined by the Duke of Windsor with his Norfolk jackets, tweed suits, Argyle sweaters and plus fours. As a form of dressing down, which suited the American preference for a relaxed and functional way of dressing, it filtered into the prestigious Northeastern colleges such as Princeton, Columbia, Yale and Harvard in the 1930s, where it became the quintessential American mode.

By the 1950s the look had become the predominant style on campus for men and women. Brooks Brothers, the main purveyor of campus fashions, introduced a women's fitting room to their stores in 1954, evidence of the appeal of their shirts to both sexes. Because it was worn by the most privileged in society, it symbolised wealth and leisure – university-affiliated sports jerseys and US army-style khaki chinos (as a tribute to the Allied victory in World War II and the grants given to veterans to go to college).

The look was also influenced by an appropriation of the sharp tailoring of jazz musicians, like Charlie Parker, and a trend for Palm Beach resort fashion, including colourful Madras shirts and loafers.

Following the ongoing Vietnam War, a sense of disillusionment in the hippie era and a return to more conservative values in the early 1970s, the All-American Ivy League style dominated once again, transitioning into the preppy style of designers like Ralph Lauren and Tommy Hilfiger. The international popularity of this style was aided by the film *Love Story* (1970). Costume designers Pearl Somner and Alice Manougian Martin dressed Ryan O'Neal and Ali MacGraw in camel coats, trench coats and checks.

In 1971 Ralph Lauren opened his first store on Rodeo Drive as his tailoring exemplified a new appreciation of luxury. He designed Robert Redford's suits in *The Great Gatsby* (1974), which sparked a

Ivy League campus fashion, early 1960s.

nostalgia for the original impeccable 1920s dandy look that had shaped Ivy League style.

Lauren became renowned for his all-American aesthetic of crisp pastel shirts, double-breasted suits and chinos. By 1981, when Polo Ralph Lauren International opened in London, the Ivy League style had truly gone mainstream. In 1978, Calvin Klein launched his first menswear range. When he followed up with underwear, jeans and scent, he would create a whole lifestyle around his preppy designs.

BLUE DENIM REBELLION

ZIP-FLY JEANS
LEE RIDER
1955

When news broke in September 1955 that actor and style icon James Dean had been killed in a car crash, it was a poignant end to a star who seemed to live a fast and reckless life. He had only had one film, *East of Eden*, released while he was alive; his second movie, *Rebel without a Cause* came out just one month after his death. Dean was heralded as a tragic hero on screen, dressed in a red windbreaker and a pair of Lee 101z Riders; a moment that marked the birth of the teenager. As Jim Stark, an angst-ridden teenager who doesn't know what he's rebelling against, Dean spoke for an entire generation of young people, and blue denim jeans became their symbol. In *Giant* (1955), his last screen appearance, James Dean again wore the fashionable Lee Riders, worn in countercultural do-it-yourself mode – faded, shrunk-to-fit and with the cuffs turned up at the bottom to showcase boots.

Lee 101z Rider jeans were the first jeans to feature a zip fly when they were launched in 1926, and while they were initially targeted at rodeo riders and cowboys, they were picked up by college students and 'dude ranch' tourists in the 1930s. While Lee Riders were Dean's preferred choice, the original, patented jeans were created almost 100 years before, by Levi Strauss, when they were known as 'work overalls'.

Levi Strauss arrived in California in 1853 to take advantage of the Gold Rush by selling products from his family's dry goods business to the pioneers heading west. Jacob Davis, a Nevada tailor, bought his cotton twill wholesale, and had begun selling indigo-dyed work trousers with copper rivets on the pockets. He approached Strauss with an idea to go into business together, and by the early 1870s they began mass-manufacturing their denims, dyed with indigo as it was cheap and fade resistant.

By the beginning of the twentieth century, they had two major competitors – Lee Jeans and the Blue Bell Overall Company, later renamed Wrangler. Their popularity was driven by the Westerns produced by Hollywood and then on television in the 1950s, which created a romanticised myth around the cowboy in his durable work clothes. World War II had also helped spread American culture abroad and, along with their depiction in Hollywood, US products became a cornerstone of prosperity and independence. The United States represented freedom and modernity, and home-grown products like Coca-Cola and denim work overalls became imbued with this same symbolism.

In the 1950s, with the promotion of comfort and material wealth as fulfilling happiness, young people in the US pushed back against mainstream society,

James Dean in Lee Rider jeans for his final movie *Giant*, 1956.

THE RISE OF THE COUNTERCULTURE 1954–1984

using music and fashion to rebel. The angst-ridden idols on screen like James Dean and Marlon Brando, and jukebox stars like Elvis Presley and Eddie Cochran, embodied the spirit of denim rebellion. Blue jeans, worn with a white T-shirt and work boots, was simple, hardwearing and rugged, except now they weren't being worn by people working on ranches – they were being worn for leisure.

Modern women also poured themselves into jeans, with stars Marilyn Monroe and Elizabeth Taylor imbuing them with a feminine sexuality, the denim clinging to and moulding their curves. 'Levi's for Ladies' had originally been introduced in the 1930s, and came pre-shrunk, but many women chose to rebel and wear shrink-to-fit men's jeans instead.

From being associated with hard work and grit, of the pioneering spirit of cowboys, jeans were now associated with danger and sex, and led to a moral panic around rock 'n' roll and movies that depicted teenagers. In *Jailhouse Rock*, Elvis Presley played up to the notion of criminal behaviour, dressed completely in denim, and in 1957 Levi's caused outrage when they released an advert featuring school pupils wearing jeans, with the slogan 'Right for School'.

Over the years, jeans lost some of their subversive appeal as they became one of the most common of wardrobe staples. But the Lee 101z Riders are forever linked with the outsider appeal of James Dean on screen. In a 1993 advertising campaign they used an image of Dean facing away from the camera, with hands in his pockets and the slogan 'worn by rebels, fit for heroes' – demonstrating an enduring relationship between rebellion and cool.

'IT'S A LITTLE STRANGE TO RISE FROM WORK CLOTHES TO HIGH FASHION, BUT WE'RE NOT FIGHTING IT.'

PETER E. HAAS, PRESIDENT OF LEVI STRAUSS, 1973

As soon as rock 'n' roll arrived in Britain in 1954 with Bill Haley's 'Shake, Rattle and Roll', teenagers were hooked on the new sound. It represented their energy, youth and rebelliousness.

The UK media was unsure what to make of this new form of music and the young fans it garnered, particularly with increased Black immigration to the country. The tabloid *Daily Mail* advised its readers: 'It is deplorable. It is tribal. And it is from America ... Rock and roll is sexy ... It has something of the African tom-tom and voodoo dance.'

Britain in the early 1950s was emerging from the post-war gloom with rationing still in place. But as television entered people's homes, an American consumer culture began to influence youth – more working-class kids were expressing themselves through fashion and music, previously seen as the privilege of the wealthy.

They looked to the modern rebels they saw on screen – disaffected anti-heroes who wore the working man uniform of jeans, T-shirt and a leather jacket. The most shocking was Johnny Strabler, Marlon Brando in *The Wild One*, the leader of a motorcycle gang who terrorized a small town. It was outrageous, dangerous – and it was banned by censors who feared it would lead British youth astray. Yet these urban cowboys in leather captured the imaginations of a generation of teens and the glamour of rock 'n' roll.

THE FIRST FASHION BOUTIQUE

BAZAAR BOUTIQUE
MARY QUANT
1955

When Mary Quant threw open the doors to London's first fashion boutique, Bazaar, in 1955, it was to a Britain that had only just emerged from wartime rationing the year before.

This exciting new retail experience in the heart of Chelsea, with jazz records pulsing from inside the shop, and an atmosphere more akin to a club than an atelier, rang in a new era of youth and self-expression. It was here that style-conscious girls could pick up Quant's signature skinny-rib sweaters, sack dresses, mini-skirts and daisy-patterned tights, as well as jewellery and accessories from specially curated mod designers.

After graduating from Goldsmiths in 1953, where she had trained to be a teacher, Quant began her career as an apprentice at a Mayfair milliner, while spending her spare time adapting paper patterns in her bedsit and selling them on to a widening circle of customers who were part of the fashionable 'Chelsea set'. Two years later, Quant and husband Alexander Plunket Greene opened Bazaar in Markham House on London's fashionable King's Road.

At first, she sold outfits that she sourced wholesale, but she was frustrated with the quality and decided to stock her own designs. She was also encouraged by the coverage she had received in *Harper's Bazaar* for a pair of her own lounge pyjamas. Her unique designs exemplified the Chelsea Look and drew on the 1920s flapper aesthetic – child-like dresses that allowed freedom of movement and came in bright colours and ever-shortening hem lengths. Her customers became known as 'dolly birds'; they were attracted to the quirky window displays, which British designer John Bates put together. Along with Quant, he would be credited with the invention of the mini-skirt.

Bazaar was one of a number of boutiques that defined the youthquake era of the 1960s, such as Biba (see pages 96–97), Granny Takes a Trip and Bus Stop, a mecca for fashion-conscious Mods who lived to spend money on the latest fashions. Growing up in a period of affluence, they had increasing independence and disposable income. Bazaar was also espoused by revered models and musicians, from Twiggy and Jean Shrimpton to Pattie Boyd and George Harrison. The King's Road and Carnaby Street were retail phenomena, particularly on Saturdays, when young people came to shop and show off their new looks. The boutique would be the first stop before going onto coffee bars and to mod nightclubs, wearing the hottest looks picked up from Bazaar, and places like it.

As Quant wrote in her 1966 autobiography, 'The young intellectual has got to learn that fashion is not frivolous; it is part of being alive today.'

Mary Quant behind the counter at Bazaar, 1960.

THE RISE OF THE COUNTERCULTURE 1954–1984

THE BOUTIQUE

By 1960, Britain had come out of the post-war gloom, where new council houses, a surge in white-collar office work and innovative technology meant social mobility was possible for anyone. As a result of the baby boom, by the sixties there was a more youthful population than ever before, and with expanded education opportunities, increasing numbers of young people enrolled in art school, where they developed skills in graphic design, art and fashion.

The concept of shopping was revolutionized by the opening of hip new boutiques, beginning with Mary Quant's Bazaar in 1955, and followed by Biba, Bus Stop and Granny Takes a Trip. Carnaby Street, previously a run-down street in Soho, and the King's Road, became the epicentres of this new retail revolution.

The shops were owned by similarly youthful, artistic entrepreneurs, who had an eye for fashion and knew how to appeal to the market with their colourful, art nouveau-inspired facades and unique window displays, with the latest records playing to draw the crowds in. A new generation of women, who worked as shop assistants or secretaries, would gather on a Saturday afternoon to spend their modest disposable income on the latest fashions, as worn by Cathy McGowan, the presenter of the hit show *Ready, Steady Go!*

One of the first to transform Carnaby Street was John Stephen, who catered to groups of teenage mods, exacting in how they wanted their suits cut. Stephen, an ambitious, young Glaswegian designer with a line of boutiques, specialised in affordable made-to-measure Italian-style suits and American Ivy League fashions. His boutiques, Mod Male, His Clothes and Male West One, were the first to have hip, trendy shop assistants modelling the clothes, who, in Stephen's words 'just smoke and lean against the wall and put records on.'

Carnaby Street and its boutiques became the focal point of Swinging London. As profiled in a famous article in *Time* magazine, it became the Number One tourist attraction besides Buckingham Palace. 'Ancient elegance and new opulence are all

Carnaby Street, London, in the swinging sixties.

tangled up in a dazzling blur of op and pop. The city is alive with birds (girls) and beatles, buzzing with minicars and telly stars, pulsing with half a dozen separate veins of excitement', it declared.

Fashionable young people could mix with idols like the Small Faces, Mick Jagger, Keith Moon and Dusty Springfield at the hippest boutiques. Granny Takes a Trip, one such fashionable King's Road boutique, was founded by graphic designer Nigel Waymouth and vintage collector Sheila Cohen in 1966. Its psychedelic interiors, like that of a New Orleans bordello, helped to shape a new foppish dandy style of velvet suits, paisley shirts, Afghan coats and floral jackets, as worn by stars like George Harrison.

By the mid-1970s, during a period of social unrest in Britain, Vivienne Westwood and Malcolm McLaren launched their own controversial boutique, which went through a series of guises, from Sex, with its name in pink rubber letters, to Seditionaries. It was where the punk movement was born.

FASHION FOR THE SPACE AGE

MOON GIRL COLLECTION
ANDRÉ COURRÈGES
1965

In 1961, the year that Russia's Yuri Gagarin became the first man in space, André Courrèges launched his streamlined mini-skirt, followed a few years later by a cutting edge collection that would reflect the new Space Age.

The French couturier was one of a group of designers, along with Pierre Cardin and Paco Rabanne, who used high-tech sports fabric as a symbol of futurism, at a time when people were getting ever closer to the moon and stars and space travel was not just a wild dream. He has also been credited as one of the inventors of the mini-skirt, along with Mary Quant.

Courrèges' revolutionary and futuristic Moon Girl collection hit the press in 1965, predating Stanley Kubrick's *2001: A Space Odyssey* by three years. With a minimalist white-and-silver aesthetic for trousers and tunics, thigh-skimming mini-skirts that were shorter than ever before, astronaut helmets, along with large white sunglasses from Rhodoid plastic and white, patent, calf-length moon boots, it was a look that completely dazzled fashion editors and buyers.

Susan Train, fashion editor of American *Vogue* in Paris, attended the landmark 1965 show with Diana Vreeland, who was a fan of Courrèges. 'The girls were sporty, tanned, jumping around and smiling,' Train recalled decades later, in 2001. It was a completely different experience to other shows. 'They were terrifically different from the solemn models that were slinking around other salons. Vreeland was just mad about Courrèges. The skirts were short compared with those of other designers. They got everyone into tunics and pants, and there was lots of white, which was such a shock.'

Courrèges was soon heralded as the future of Paris fashion, with *Women's Wear Daily* referring to him as the 'Le Corbusier of Paris couture', for his geometric shapes made from inventive, novel materials. Artist Andy Warhol offered profuse admiration on how Courrèges' clothes were so 'beautiful. Everyone should look the same, dressed in silver.'

Courrèges had fine-tuned his craft with a decade spent at Cristóbal Balenciaga. In 1961 he launched his own label, using the meticulous cutting skills he'd learned from the master craftsman. He described his concern in working to 'harmoniously resolve functional problems, just like the engineer who designs a plane'.

Courrèges was assisted by his wife, Coqueline, in inventing this new vision of white tunics, trousers and boots, which they hoped would supplant jeans in popularity. In 2001, Coqueline described how they were inspired by the 'generation of the year 2000. What we imagined would come in the future and

Andre Courrèges' Moon Girl look, 1965.

what we would encounter. The first confirmation of our vision was when man walked on the moon in 1969.'

He used thick gabardine because it held its shape and he also developed a signature double-welt seam, which he described as 'pencil strokes in the sketch', to add to the resistance of the cloth. It created a sense of stability, just as astronauts were protected and encased in their suits. His Moon Girls, in cute helmets that tied under the chin, with their bug-eyed glasses and flat boots that allowed them to jump and skip, were unnervingly youthful.

While Courrèges' tailoring was complex, his other concepts from the collection, such as the white sunglasses and his white go-go boots, or 'kinky' boots, were endlessly imitated by other, cheaper brands. An article in *The Sunday People*, in November 1965, stated: 'You see them in the shopping queue. You see them climbing the steps of a bus. They have even been seen at a Buckingham Palace garden party. And the more you see them, the angrier gets Frenchman André Courrèges – the man who first designed them.'

To try to get ahead of the pirating of his designs, he sold a share of his business to L'Oréal to expand his ready-to-wear lines, but by 1969, when man finally landed on the moon, the hippie phenomenon was in full flow, and his own aesthetic a symbol of another age.

'WE WERE INSPIRED BY THE GENERATION OF THE YEAR 2000. WHAT WE IMAGINED WOULD COME IN THE FUTURE AND WHAT WE WOULD ENCOUNTER. THE FIRST CONFIRMATION OF OUR VISION WAS WHEN MAN WALKED ON THE MOON IN 1969.'

COQUELINE COURRÈGES

Mods dancing, 1965.

From its origins in London's Soho jazz clubs, the mod movement became the premiere youth subculture in the first half of the 1960s. The 'mod' label was given to anything that was cool, modern and quirky – from Mary Quant mini-dresses and the geometric Vidal Sassoon bob to op art, Terence Conran design and Andrés Courrèges' Space Age couture. But the original mod style referenced American Ivy League fashions, the style of jazz musician idols like Charlie Parker, and imbued it with European flare: an appreciation for Italian coffee, Gauloises cigarettes, Jean-Paul Sartre and boxy jackets known as 'bum freezers'.

Mods set their own trends by custom-making their suits from specialist tailors. Their disposable income was spent on the right clothes, the coolest records and buying accessories for their Vespa scooters. The 'faces' were the most fashionable, leading the trends, while the 'tickets', from the Beatles song 'Ticket to Ride' copied these styles. Following the success of 'My Generation', The Who became the voice of the movement. Pete Townshend in a 1968 interview with *Rolling Stone* summed up the style as hip, fashionable, clean, groovy.

METALLIC MANIA

MANIFESTO: TWELVE UNWEARABLE DRESSES IN CONTEMPORARY MATERIALS
PACO RABANNE
1966

Paco Rabanne may have branded his 1966 collection Manifesto: Twelve Unwearable Dresses in Contemporary Materials, but his mini-dresses in moulded plastics, hammered metal and knitted fur became some of the most coveted pieces of fashion. He was also way ahead of his time in his use of recyclable material, with his paper dresses.

Rabanne's plastic and metal sheaths were famously constructed with pliers and glue, and the designer later sold DIY kits with discs, rings and pliers for people to try for themselves.

Born Francisco Rabaneda y Cuervo in 1934 in the Basque region of Spain, Rabanne and his mother, the head seamstress for Cristóbal Balenciaga, fled to France during the Spanish Civil War (1936–1939). After changing his name to Paco Rabanne, he used his skills from his studies as an architect to construct couture from modern industrial materials. He emerged on the fashion scene at a time when designers like Pierre Cardin and André Courrèges were inspired by the Space Age to make their futuristic designs.

His first collection in 1964, entitled Twelve Experimental Dresses, was followed by Manifesto in 1966, which was shown at the Hotel Georges V in Paris. It featured sheath dresses constructed from Rhodoid (cellulose acetate plastic) over sheer fabric and mini-dresses from iridescent plastic discs, all worn without underwear or any shoes. This show also broke with convention by using music to soundtrack the show and by casting women of colour as models. These futuristic designs earned him the nickname the 'Jules Verne of couture', while Vogue dubbed him the 'talk of Paris'.

Chanteuse Françoise Hardy chose to wear a mini-dress constructed from gold plates inlaid with diamonds, and when style icon Audrey Hepburn, known for her more conservative appreciation of Givenchy couture, wore a metal paillette dress in the film Two for the Road (1967), she brought Rabanne's designs to international attention. The following year, Rabanne designed the futuristic costumes for Jane Fonda's sci-fi heroine Barbarella.

Such was the impact of his collection, he found that his creations were being ripped off and mass-produced, much like designers experience now. There was a particular trend for copies of the disc-shaped plastic jewellery that accessorized his dresses. The Times reported: 'You can buy the genuine Rabanne article over here (at a price) but you can also buy very attractive and effective copies and pieces of jewelry in plastic or cellophane, which are "inspired" by Rabanne for very much less. And why not?'

Paco Rabanne in his studio, 1966.

THE RISE OF THE COUNTERCULTURE 1954–1984

SUBVERSIVE SUITS

LE SMOKING
YVES SAINT LAURENT
1966

Yves Saint Laurent referenced Marlene Dietrich and lesbian culture in 1920s Paris with the launch of his revolutionary Le Smoking suits in 1966. It was officially the first tuxedo designed for women, and worn with high heels, it made a strong statement that the wearer was daring, provocative and sexually powerful. Le Smoking was designed to fit a woman's body, was well-tailored and tinged with sexuality. Even so, the cutting-edge design was met with only a whimper at its first showing, with reportedly only one suit sold.

Saint Laurent persisted with his style, bringing it back to the catwalk for his next collection. As *The New York Times* reported on 3 February 1967: 'Pass the message to Marlene Dietrich: Yves Saint Laurent is a fan. The spring–summer collection Saint Laurent showed to the press this morning was drenched with a Dietrich-of-the-nineteen-thirties look ...'

The models paraded down the catwalk in gangster-striped, wide-legged trouser suits with broad lapels, completed with fedoras. Watching the show were Yves Saint Laurent's muses, three of the chicest, coolest women of the time – Catherine Deneuve, Elsa Martinelli and Françoise Hardy, the 'Yé-Yé girl' who wore the Le Smoking suit as part of her edgy, streamlined look, making it impossible to ignore. Following the 1967 show, fashion writer Gloria Emerson described Le Smoking as being 'for the young, young woman who knows how to speak with a cigarette stuck in her mouth'.

John T. Molloy's *Dress for Success* (1975) was a landmark book that set out clear codes for how women could be taken seriously in the workplace. He advised women not to draw attention to their sexuality, nor to appear too masculine, as this could be threatening to men. Molloy wrote: 'My research indicates that a three-piece pinstriped suit not only does not add to a woman's authority, it destroys it. It makes her look like an "imitation man" and that always fails.'

Despite warnings about the masculine nature of the suit, the YSL tuxedo became the precursor to 1980s power dressing for women in business, and the designer included a version for each of his collections until 2002. Madonna paid tribute to Le Smoking in the 'Express Yourself' music video, demonstrating how the tuxedo on a woman was subversive and powerful. It was also the epitome of style. As Yves Saint Laurent put it: 'For a woman, the tuxedo is an indispensable garment in which she will always feel in style, for it is a stylish garment and not a fashionable garment. Fashions fade, style is eternal.'

Yves Saint Laurent's Le Smoking, 1967.

THE RISE OF THE COUNTERCULTURE 1954–1984

BONNIE FEVER

THE BONNIE AND CLYDE LOOK
THEADORA VAN RUNKLE
1967

When *Time* magazine featured Arthur Penn's *Bonnie and Clyde* on its front cover, in December 1967, launching a new wave of American cinema, the public and critics paid attention. Its stylised violence broke with conventions and marked the end of Hollywood's studio system and its censorship codes. But what made the biggest impact was the glamour of the Depression-era outlaws, with Faye Dunaway and Warren Beauty as beautiful, anti-establishment heroes in costumes designed by Theadora Van Runkle. The pin-stripe suits of Clyde and the berets, tight sweaters, neckties and midi-skirts of Bonnie offered a counterpoint to the current late 1960s trends for fluoro prints and synthetic micro-minis.

It was the first film that Van Runkle had worked on as costume designer, but she created such excitement with her designs for the film that she became an overnight sensation, sparking a dramatic drop in hem lengths and a new lease of life to the beret industry. The designer said: 'The minute I read the first page I saw everything. I knew it was going to be fabulous.' She credited the success of the look, because 'they wore clothes that people could wear to work and wear in their real lives'.

The costumes tapped into the fashion for a nostalgic view of the 1930s, and the anger young people felt with the government at the height of the Vietnam War, civil rights protests and the feminist movement. They felt sympathies for the criminals in the movie who seemed to be fighting against an unfair society and a repressive government.

Bonnie Parker, who threw on her clothes without a bra, represented freedom and emancipation, and her calf-length skirts sparked a shift from thigh-skimming skirts to hems that hovered above the ground. Van Runkle used a bias cut so that the dresses would swing and paired ankle-length midi-skirts with tailored jackets – a look that meant business in the office, or for robbing a bank.

The beret experienced a surge in popularity due to the film. Production in the French town of Lourdes reportedly went from 5,000 to 12,000 each week. Van Runkle commented that, 'The beret was the final culmination of the silhouette ...Without the beret it would have been charming, but not the same.'

Bonnie Fever swept through Paris and London in 1967, with Faye Dunaway snapped on the King's Road in a beret and midi-skirt. At the Paris premiere, she was greeted by a crowd of thousands in their own berets, neckties and midi-skirts. Brigitte Bardot was so enamoured with the Bonnie look that she

Faye Dunaway in Theadora Van Runkle's costumes for *Bonnie and Clyde*.

THE RISE OF THE COUNTERCULTURE 1954–1984

appeared in the video for 'Bonnie and Clyde', her duet with Serge Gainsbourg, in 1968, with aesthetics lifted straight from the movie – a beret, blonde bob and machine gun.

As fashion's current dream girl, Dunaway also appeared on the cover of *Life* magazine on 12 January 1968, modelling the style. The accompanying article noted that 'she has a firm opinion on skirt lengths: she wants them very mini or truly midi, the new mid-calf length that the '30s revival is bringing back.'

On the back of the surge in interest for the Bonnie Parker's midi-skirt, mini-skirts were banned in the *Women's Wear Daily* offices. 'We all know minis are dead,' explained the memo in 1968, which was circulated to staff.

Vogue editor-in-chief Diana Vreeland defended the mini-skirt, which she said 'looks delicious in the summer with the right legs and the right girl'. This battle between the skirt lengths was soon dubbed 'the hemline war'. The midi-skirt offered freedom to women who perhaps felt they didn't have the 'right legs', and allowed them to dress for themselves rather than for men. But other women found them to be dowdy and unflattering and revolted against the fashion industry for dictating to women what they should and shouldn't wear.

The New Yorker warned that 'no amount of protest will stem the tide of the longer skirt', and on many shop floors in 1970, the midi-skirt, along with the flowing maxi, seemed to be the only skirts to be found on racks.

In 1970, *Show* magazine reflected: 'Probably no one imagined at the time that the most far-reaching contribution *Bonnie and Clyde* would leave to our acid-rock-pop generation was its influence on fashion. Nor that Theadora Van Runkle … would become responsible for the midis and braless bosoms that are the trademark of the early seventies. But that's just what happened.'

'PROBABLY NO ONE IMAGINED AT THE TIME THAT THE MOST FAR-REACHING CONTRIBUTION BONNIE AND CLYDE WOULD LEAVE TO OUR ACID-ROCK-POP GENERATION WAS ITS INFLUENCE ON FASHION.'

SHOW MAGAZINE, 1970

San Francisco hippies
in the 1960s.

Hippies emerged in 1965 in the Haight-Ashbury area of San Francisco, as a response to new upheavals in society, including the Vietnam War, nuclear armament and the sexual revolution. They expressed their sense of social consciousness through folk and rock music, and with their turned-on, tuned-out, dropped-out ethos, they created their own communities and tripped on acid. These mind-bending drugs in turn influenced a desire for clashing swirls of purples and orange and bohemian clothing, which served as a counteraction to war and civil rights protests.

With a rallying cry for young people to arrive in San Francisco with 'a flower in their hair', as the Scott McKenzie song went, thousands of hopefuls arrived in the city to discover the peace, love and LSD for themselves. A new form of poster art, inspired by art nouveau, Dada and pop art, flourished with artists like Rick Griffin, Stanley Mouse and Alton Kelley creating posters for festivals and covers for LPs.

As the war in Vietnam escalated and Americans were drafted to fight overseas, young people took part in anti-war protests, sit-ins and student strikes. Huge open air music festivals attracted immense crowds, such as January 1967's the Human Be-In in Golden Gate Park, sparking the Summer of Love. By 1967, psychedelia was replacing the mod fashion of Swinging London. Hair was grown longer and worn more freely and ethnic-style clothing replaced the streamlined, modernist look.

THE BIBA 'TOTAL LOOK'

THE BIBA DEPARTMENT STORE
BARBARA HULANICKI
1973

When it opened its doors, in September 1973, to great fanfare, the Biba department store on Kensington High Street was the must-see place of the moment. It was a treasure trove of jars of fake ostrich plumes, piles of plush velvet cushions, leopard-print sofas and racks of women's clothing coded by colour. Everything was *Velvet Goldmine* kitsch and art nouveau luxe. The fashion emporium epitomized Swinging London.

The Biba label was founded by fashion designer Barbara Hulanicki, when she was still in her twenties, along with her advertiser husband Steven Fitz-Simon. They had used their expertise to completely reinvent the shopping experience, originally with their small Abingdon Road store in 1964. It had become a mod meeting place, which provided a taste of luxury to the young woman on her shop assistant or secretary wages. Described as the 'Total Look', it was funky, sexy and nostalgic.

On the back of their huge success, the couple made the bold decision to take over the art deco Derry & Toms department store, with their complete remodel said to cost around 11 million dollars. The great expense of the building meant it was a considerable gamble. But the 'Total Look' had been revolutionary, in that customers could match their Biba clothes with their accessories, their make-up and even their bed linen. It offered affordable clothing for girls on any budget, who could dress like Twiggy, Anita Pallenberg and Marianne Faithful.

What the Biba department store created was a new concept in shopping that would be an influential template on how to drive excitement in young people. Alwyn W. Turner, in *Biba: The Biba Experience*, described it as: 'the concept of shopping as an experience, a leisure activity for the young … It was no longer something that a girl did reluctantly with her mother. It was a social event in its own right to be shared with peers.'

Just two years after opening, the department store was forced to close, after the property group British Land, which had a 75 per cent stake in Biba, announced it had lost £1,460,000. The flamboyant psychedelia that had captured the youthful excitement of the 1960s seemed less relevant in the cash-strapped mid-1970s, at a time when Britain was experiencing the worst inflation in Europe.

A Texas sales assistant, Michelle Braverman, recalled strolling down Madison Avenue on a wintry day in the early 1970s, dressed in a maxi-coat and a cloche hat that she had bought from Biba. She noticed that an attractive woman who was walking past her could not take her eyes off the hat. 'She was Ali MacGraw, and she was with Bob Evans. You don't forget things like that. And you don't forget Biba.'

Twiggy at Biba's department store, 1971.

THE RISE OF THE COUNTERCULTURE 1954–1984

ZIGGY STARDUST

ZIGGY STARDUST
KANSAI YAMAMOTO
1973

When Kansai Yamamoto flew to New York in 1973 to watch David Bowie perform at Radio City Music Hall for the Ziggy Stardust tour, it was the first time he'd seen his own flamboyant designs for Bowie in action, and he was struck by the sensational effect on the audience. 'It was very dramatic, and the audience all rose to their feet, so there was a standing ovation right at the beginning,' he recalled.

For his million-selling album *The Rise and Fall of Ziggy Stardust and the Spiders from Mars*, Bowie's concept for his alter-ego Ziggy Stardust was an alien rock star sent to Earth as a messenger. To fully inhabit this vision, he commissioned the Japanese designer to create all the androgynous and futuristic designs, to add to the red mullet hair, the kabuki make-up and the gold astral sphere on his forehead, visualised by make-up artist Pierre La Roche.

The son of a tailor, Kansai Yamamoto was born in 1944 in Yokohama, Japan. He moved to London where he held his debut show at London Fashion Week in 1971, the first time a Japanese designer had shown his collection there. While Japanese fashion was often associated with minimalism and wabi-sabi, celebrating simplicity and imperfection, Kansai followed the 'basara' aesthetic, where he was inspired by the imperial court robes of Japan, kabuki theatre costumes and Japanese art, in creating his colourful designs. 'Basara means to dress freely, with a stylish extravagance,' he said in 2013. 'It is colourful and flamboyant and it lies at the heart of my design.'

Bowie noticed Kansai's work on the cover of *Harpers & Queen* in 1971 and, after buying a couple of his pieces from a shop on the King's Road, commissioned the designer to create costumes for his 1972 tour. 'I approached Bowie's clothes as if I was designing for a female,' Kansai said. His gender-fluid costumes provoked countless imitators, leading to a movement of punky glam-rock teenagers copying the hair, the make-up and the Lurex leotards.

After Bowie killed off Ziggy Stardust in July 1973, he continued to collaborate with Kansai for his next alter-ego, Aladdin Sane, which included one of his most famous looks, a patent black-and-white jumpsuit with bowed legs. By the 1980s, the designer brought his fashion shows to stadium-sized audiences which he called 'Kansai Super Shows', combining fashion, music, acrobatics and Japanese theatre. A crowd of 120,000 attended his 1993 Moscow Red Square event, proving that his vision was as groundbreaking on its own as it was with Bowie.

David Bowie as Ziggy Stardust, 1973.

THE FASHION DUEL

THE BATTLE OF VERSAILLES
AMERICAN V FRENCH DESIGNERS
1973

Hailed as the night American fashion finally received the recognition it deserved, the Battle of Versailles was a fashion show held at the Palace of Versailles, where French couturiers faced off with US designers, in front of an audience of such luminaries as Grace Kelly, Marie-Hélène de Rothschild, Jane Birkin and Andy Warhol.

The concept, the brainchild of publicist Eleanor Lambert and curator of Versailles Gerald Van der Kemp, was a benefit event to raise 60 million dollars for the much-needed restoration of the palace.

Paris had long been the fashion capital of the world, and design houses were steeped in tradition and a sense of entitlement that their couture was superior. American designers were typically dismissed as merely purveyors of sportswear for their more accessible ready-to-wear lines. It was a clash of cultures as French designers Yves Saint Laurent, Pierre Cardin, Emanuel Ungaro, Marc Bohan and Hubert de Givenchy competed against the American designers Oscar de la Renta, Stephen Burrows, Halston, Bill Blass and Anne Klein.

For their section of the show, the French created a glittering set featuring Cinderella's pumpkin carriage, from which models in Dior alighted, and with performances by dancers from Crazy Horse, ballet dancer Rudolf Nureyev and Josephine Baker. Liza Minnelli, a close friend of Halston, performed for the American half, in a number choreographed by her godmother Kay Thompson, to 'Bonjour Paris' from *Funny Face*.

The US designers arrived in Paris on a private jet packed with their couture, and fuelled by champagne, they rehearsed their performances in draughty Versailles rooms. There was diva behaviour and sniping, with Kay Thompson storming out in frustration at the models not concentrating on her instructions, and Liza Minnelli, who had recently won an Oscar for *Cabaret*, refusing to share the stage with actress Raquel Welch. Halston infuriated the other designers by referring to himself in the third person. Working as Anne Klein's assistant was a six-months-pregnant Donna Karan, who was to take over as head designer for Klein's brand, following her death from breast cancer the following year.

Further disaster struck when the Americans measured the Theatre Gabriel stage (where Marie Antoinette had once taken part in amateur performances) in feet and inches rather than in meters, leaving empty space around the set design and space. Nevertheless Liza Minnelli brought the house down with her performance, instantly sparking life into the prestigious audience. The curtain rose on the 36 American models, all dressed in street clothes, and each designer

Bethann Hardison in Halston at the Versailles fashion show.

THE RISE OF THE COUNTERCULTURE 1954–1984

showcased their looks, from Halston's dramatic Studio 54 evening gowns to Klein's sportswear and Oscar de la Renta's elegant chiffon and satin.

The show was also groundbreaking as ten Black models took part in the American half of the show, unprecedented in terms of representation. The models, including Alva Chinn, Billie Blair and Pat Cleveland, brought a fresh and very American attitude to the shows, in easy Halston chiffons that captured the spirit of the modern, active woman. 'We brought a certain vibrancy to the shows,' Pat Cleveland later told *The Cut*.

Countess Jacqueline de Ribes, who was in the audience, described how 'the French were pompous and pretentious.' She said: 'The American show was so full of life, of color. I went backstage and bought a green Oscar de la Renta dress right off the back of a model.'

The headline in *The New York Times* on 30 November, 1973 proclaimed: 'Fashion at Versailles: French Were Good, Americans Were Great.' The show was considered the moment that placed US designers firmly on the map, paving a way for the functional creations of Ralph Lauren and Tommy Hilfiger, and the later influence of designers like Marc Jacobs. The show also inspired French designers to diversify their models, with Givenchy visiting California to hire Black models for his shows, despite the resistance of some of his clients.

'FASHION AT VERSAILLES: FRENCH WERE GOOD, AMERICANS WERE GREAT.'

THE NEW YORK TIMES

Studio 54, 1978.

Built on euphoric beats, glamour and glitz, disco began as an underground movement in 1970s Manhattan, acting as a celebration of gay rights following the 1969 Stonewall riots. David Mancuso's The Loft, opened in 1970, is considered the birthplace of disco, where different races, classes and sexualities could converge. Throughout the decade there was an explosion of new nightclubs in Manhattan, including Studio 54, which promoted self-expression in how people dressed. *Vogue* said at the start of the decade: 'There are no rules in the fashion game now. You're playing it and you make up the game as you go.'

Diane von Furstenberg's wrap dress was one of the hottest items of the 1970s, selling more than five million by 1976. Wrapping around the body like a dressing gown, it could be worn from the office straight to the disco. Halston, a regular at Studio 54, with Liza Minnelli and Bianca Jagger, captured the freedom of disco with his easy designs, including his popular halterneck jersey dress.

As *The New York Times* wrote on 30 December 1979: 'The slinky, stretchy looks of body-conscious clothes became, in those throbbing environs, the "in" garb; so did vivid, acid look-at-me colours. This mania coincided with the rage for dance and sports, the ultimate goal being the lean, taut gymnast physique.'

BREAKING BARRIERS ON *VOGUE*

FIRST BLACK MODEL ON THE COVER OF *VOGUE*
BEVERLY JOHNSON
1974

In 1974, Beverly Johnson broke the fashion glass ceiling by becoming the first person of colour to ever appear on the cover of American *Vogue*, in its eight decades of circulation.

She was only twenty-one years old when she helped to create one of fashion's landmark moments. The portrait by Francesco Scavullo depicted Johnson as girl-next-door, in a blue sweater and Bulgari earrings, rather than as an exotic 'other'. It was a vision of natural, real beauty, which didn't try to hide her Blackness.

Growing up in Buffalo, New York, Johnson trained as a competitive swimmer, before studying political science at Northeastern University. While there, she began doing modelling for *Glamour* magazine. After Ford Models initially rejected her, Johnson was signed up to the prominent modelling agency led by Eileen Ford after they saw the number of assignments she was receiving. She walked the runway for Halston, performed in a commercial for National Airlines and appeared on the cover of *Glamour* six times, but when she asked the legendary Eileen Ford when she could expect her *Vogue* cover, she was dismissed.

Johnson approached modelling with an 'athlete's mind-set' and appearing on the cover of *Vogue* was like winning a gold medal at the Olympics. So instead of giving up her goal, she switched to Wilhelmina Cooper's agency.

'I didn't realize the cultural and historical significance of this cover until it hit the newsstands in August 1974,' Johnson told *Vogue* in September 2009. As soon as the edition came out, she was inundated with requests for interviews from outlets and the history-making edition sold out quickly.

There were other working Black models, including Naomi Sims and Helen Williams, and Donyale Luna was the first Black model to be pictured on the cover of British *Vogue* in 1966, but to Johnson's surprise no Black model had appeared on the more influential American *Vogue*, considered the pinnacle of achievement in modelling. In the United States, there was still a reluctance to cast women of colour, as the magazine believed that their 350,000 readers weren't ready to see a non-white model on the cover. *The New York Times*, in 1975, was quick to acknowledge that it had to do with looking 'acceptable' to white audiences, 'Beverly in an Afro, it's safe to say, would never have made the cover of *Vogue*.'

Johnson found that while she was considered groundbreaking, she was also thought of as not Black enough. As a 1975 profile in *The New York Times* put it: 'She looks, in the words of another black model, "like a white woman dipped in

Beverly Johnson on the cover of American *Vogue*, August 1974.

brown paint".' Johnson, the article stated, insisted that she didn't see herself as a Black model, rather a model who happened to be Black.

As well as moving into acting and writing a number of beauty books, Johnson used her new-found fame as a *Vogue* cover star and supermodel to campaign for equal civil rights and to encourage other Black models to follow in her footsteps. But despite Johnson's landmark place in history, the path into high fashion was still a struggle for many women of colour. The next Black model to appear on the cover of American *Vogue* wasn't until three years later, in 1977. US model and icon Grace Jones wrote in her memoirs that Beverly Johnson was the reason she left the States, 'one black model was all they needed and I would pick up the crumbs'.

In the decades since, Naomi Campbell, Iman and Tyra Banks established themselves as some of the most powerful women in the fashion industry. In 2019, *Pudding* reporter Malaika Handa analysed nineteen years of American *Vogue* covers to reveal that of the 262 cover models, only five were dark-skinned, with three of those covers belonging to actress Lupita Nyong'o. While there is a still a way to go in increasing diversity in the fashion industry, the influence of models like Winnie Harlow and Alek Wek, and the promotion of Edward Enninful as the first Black editor of British *Vogue*, demonstrate that the industry has come a long way since Beverly Johnson's groundbreaking cover.

'I DIDN'T REALIZE THE CULTURAL AND HISTORICAL SIGNIFICANCE OF THIS COVER UNTIL IT HIT THE NEWSSTANDS IN AUGUST 1974.'

BEVERLY JOHNSON

When the music video to Blondie's 'Rapture' was released, featuring artist Jean-Michel Basquiat and Fab Five Freddy, it reflected the fusion of new wave, punk, hip-hop and art in the downtown scene in New York in the late 1970s and early 1980s.

A burgeoning hip-hop scene had grown out of the South Bronx from the early 1970s, which incorporated four elements – DJing, MCing, breakdancing and graffiti. In 1973, *New York* magazine called graffiti art 'the first genuine teenage street culture since the fifties'. The figures who spray-painted across the city on service stops, buildings and subway cars became legends from the tags they left behind, soon attracting the attention of art gallery owners.

Jean-Michel Basquiat, using the tag Samo, would go from homelessness to international art stardom as he became an integral figure in Andy Warhol's circle, firstly displaying images of his tags and later abstract paintings, which he often created while dressed in Armani suits. In 1979, Basquiat launched his own clothing line, Man Made, which captured the hybrid of art and fashion, punk and hip-hop, which designer Stephen Sprouse would similarly be inspired by.

Vivienne Westwood and Malcolm McLaren had showed some of their early punk designs at the Chelsea Hotel, capturing the attention of bands like the New York Dolls. In the 1980s, on a second visit to the city, McLaren was inspired by the hip-hop movement to release 'Buffalo Gals', with a video featuring the Rock Steady Crew. The downtown movement would shape Westwood and McLaren's 1983 Witches collection. The fusion of punk and hip-hop, together with the art of Keith Haring and Basquiat, would represent a melting pot of creativity in New York in the early 1980s.

ANARCHY THROUGH DESIGN

THE BONDAGE SUIT
VIVIENNE WESTWOOD AND MALCOLM MCLAREN
1976

Vivienne Westwood and Malcolm McLaren launched a style revolution in the early 1970s with their anti-establishment punk clothing, sold from their London King's Road shop. Their bondage suit, showcased for their spring–summer 1976 collection was characteristic of their trailblazing punk style. Created in red tartan fabric, black cotton or shiny black sateen, it featured bondage straps between the knees and zippers on the crotch, as an extension of the sado-masochistic subculture they were fascinated by.

'I got so intrigued when I started to make clothes in rubber-wear by all those fetish people and the motives behind what they did ... I wanted to make exactly what they wore ... that's where all the straps and things came from,' Westwood explained.

As well as fetish-wear, the androgynous suit borrowed from army jumpsuits and motorcyclist clothing. The straps also created the effect of a straight jacket, playing on the notions of insanity, chaos and anarchy so central to the punk ethos. According to McLaren, these 'bondage kecks', became 'a declaration of war against the consumerist fashions of the High Street'.

The King's Road shop underwent a number of names and reinventions. Too Fast to Live, Too Young to Die from 1972, was a tribute to rockers and Teddy boys; SEX, from 1974 to 1976, turned to fetish-wear and shocking swastika symbolism; and for 1977, the year of the Queen's Silver Jubilee, the bondage suit was sold from Seditionaries, which Westwood said 'was making clothes for heroes and encouraging sedition – seducing into revolt'.

Punk came at a time when Britain was suffering an economic collapse and mass strikes; disaffected youth began to gather at the shop, looking for an outlet for their anger and creativity. It was here that the Sex Pistols were formed from a group of teenagers who gathered there – Sid Vicious, Johnny Rotten, Steve Jones, Paul Cook. The punk look spread through Britain's hot summer of 1976 and into 1977, with the Sex Pistols' anarchic anthem, 'God Save the Queen', its soundtrack; its artwork of the Queen, with a safety-pin through her lip, was the image of the Silver Jubilee.

The anti-establishment message of punk provoked moral indignation in the press, but for rebellious young people it was outrageously irresistible. For something that was shockingly unwearable, the bondage suit became a symbol of youthful anarchy, as well as BDSM culture.

Punks Simon Barker and Jordan modeling Seditionaries' bondage suits, 1977.

THE RISE OF THE COUNTERCULTURE 1954–1984

THE SLOGAN TEE

THE SLOGAN T-SHIRT
KATHARINE HAMNETT
1984

When Katharine Hamnett confronted Margaret Thatcher at a Downing Street reception in 1984 with the words '58% Don't Want Pershing' emblazoned across her chest, she brought slogan T-shirts into the public consciousness. The words referred to the US's Pershing and Cruise missiles moving to UK soil; and they demonstrated how a T-shirt carrying a simple message could become one of the most powerful tools for protest.

At first Hamnett had been reluctant to meet the Conservative PM, who she detested for her spending cuts. But aware that she could make an attention-grabbing statement in front of a crowd of press photographers, the British designer knocked up a silk T-shirt on the day, with big block letters inspired by tabloid headlines.

The invention of the multicolour screen-printing machine in the 1960s made it much easier and cost-effective for people to make their own T-shirts. Rock 'n' roll fans wore the tongue-and-lips tee created by John Pasche for the Rolling Stones, while Vivienne Westwood and Malcolm McLaren made their shocking, anarchic tees for the punk movement in the early 1970s.

It was Hamnett who really brought the slogan tee into the spotlight though. Fresh out of Saint Martin's School of Art, she launched her own label in 1979 with a series of T-shirts for her ready-to-wear collection. Her first slogan T-shirt in 1983 provoked discussion on the environment – others included 'Worldwide Nuclear Ban', 'Save the Sea', 'Save the World', 'Stop Acid Rain'. Hamnett's concepts were quickly picked up by pop culture, with Wham! wearing a 'Choose Life' tee in their 'Wake Me Up Before You Go Go' video. By 1984, she was selling her designs in 700 retail outlets across 40 countries.

Despite its simplicity, the slogan T-shirt can be a potent method of delivering a controversial statement that's difficult to turn away from. On meeting Thatcher, Hamnett opened her jacket so that all the photographers in the room could capture the scene. The photo was picked up and splashed on papers and has forever been remembered as a savvy use of fashion to disseminate a political message around the world.

Katharine Hamnett confronting Margaret Thatcher at Downing Street, 1984.

THE RISE OF THE COUNTERCULTURE 1954–1984

NEW ROMANTICS

In London's Covent Garden in 1979 a crowd of art students, punks and individualists gathered at the Blitz Club, where the music was electronic and new wave, and the dress code was eccentric fancy dress, from pirates to eighteenth-century fops and heroines.

The Blitz was the hottest underground nightclub in London, where the strict door policy was overseen by Steve Strange, and Boy George worked the cloak room. It was a place where punks, soul fans and drag queens would outdo one another in their outré fashions, and where the anthem was David Bowie's 'Heroes'; they were heroes for being brave enough to express themselves in attention-grabbing get-up.

The guests, who became known as the Blitz Kids, adapted their clothes from vintage pieces gleaned from charity shops, stitching together their elaborate outfits, or purchased them from Covent Garden shop PX, to transform into Jacobites in tartan, Pierrot clowns, swashbucklers in frilled blouses and Victorian goths. Writer Beverley Glick, in *Sounds*, in September 1980, coined the name the 'New Romantics', in reference to Romantic poets like Byron and Shelley, who they dressed in tribute to.

Some of the up-and-coming names at the Blitz included milliner Stephen Jones, designer John Galliano, DJ Jeremy Healy, Sade, Keren Woodward from Bananarama and Gary Kemp from Spandau Ballet, a band whose aesthetics were very much influenced by the creativity of the movement.

'From the foppish fashions of the video boom to the repetitive beats of house and techno, the whole of the Eighties was prefigured in the bitchy brew of Blitz,' wrote Dave Rimmer in his book on the New Romantics.

The media quickly caught on and images of this cult of clubbers were splashed across magazines and newspapers. Some of the Blitz Kids even appeared in the music video for their hero David Bowie's 'Ashes to Ashes'. It seemed as if a sense of style had returned to London. 'We're making people realize that Britain has got something happening again which has been missing, I think anyway,' said Strange in 1982. And

New Romantics at Camden Palace, 1980.

perhaps that was true: the New Romantics appeared at a turning point in British history – when Margaret Thatcher was elected in 1979 and the nation became obsessed with consumerism and privatisation.

Eventually the movement became a victim of its own success, and with too many people clambering to get into the club, the Blitz was closed in October 1980, just as Spandau Ballet and Steve Strange's Visage released their first singles, 'To Cut a Long Story Short' and 'Fade to Grey' respectively.

It may have been short-lived, but the New Romantics would shape the synth-pop sounds of Human League, Soft Cell and Duran Duran, and held a lasting legacy in Princess Diana's pie-crust collars and elaborately-frilled wedding dress. It also directly inspired Vivienne Westwood's Pirates collection, with designs that referenced the swagger of seafarers in loose shirts and bicorn hats, and a label that stated 'Clothes for Heroes'.

FASHION GRAFFITI

THE GRAFFITI COLLECTION
STEPHEN SPROUSE
1984

Three thousand people crammed into New York's Ritz nightclub to witness Stephen Sprouse's first major show. His autumn–winter 1984 collection was the hottest ticket in town, as models in blonde wigs and dark glasses showcased 1960s-inspired Day-glo wool cardigans, bodysuits and sequinned mini-dresses covered in graffiti. The clothes had a rock-star swagger to them, and his influences were Edie Sedgwick and the Velvet Underground, Jim Morrison and the Stones.

In April 1983, when his first collection debuted, Sprouse was catapulted to fame, with his clothes appearing in major fashion publications like *Vogue*, *Harper's Bazaar* and *Women's Wear Daily*. John Duka, *The New York Times*' fashion correspondent wrote at the time that Sprouse's clothes are the first 'in years to tap into the currents of popular culture and to translate the drive of rock music and MTV videos into retail form'.

Sprouse was at the heart of New York street culture, taking inspiration from pop art and the downtown scene in the early 1980s. He lived in the same apartment block as Debbie Harry, who chose to wear one of his designs – a silk asymmetrical dress printed with television static – for Blondie's 'Heart of Glass' video. He became friends with Andy Warhol, whose spirit was evident throughout Sprouse's collections. Sprouse was to fashion what Jean-Michel Basquiat and Keith Haring were to art, reflecting the subcultural collision of 1980s New York.

Sprouse, who was born in Ohio in 1953, began his career working under Halston; the designer who defined the Studio 54 glitz. Sprouse launched his own collection in 1983, where he created fine tailoring covered with graffiti print, inspired by the tagging craze of the hip-hop scene across the city. He initially used marker pens to scribble across the chiffons and neon jackets, contrasting the grimy tags that were branded across New York's subways and walls with luxury silks, cashmeres and sequins.

In 1988 he launched a new collection in collaboration with street artist Keith Haring, but despite its acclaim, he continued to lose money and was forced to close his label. Considered the 'Great American Fashion Designer Who Never Quite Was', his graffiti collection was given new life fifteen years later. In 2001, Marc Jacobs, a long-time fan, asked Sprouse to collaborate on a revised version of the Louis Vuitton Speedy bag, using the graffiti print from his original collection. 'I loved his clothes, I was a real fan,' Jacobs said. 'They were just really cool New York kind of clothes.' The Sprouse-inspired bag was a phenomenal success, becoming one of the 'It' bags of the 2000s.

Stephen Sprouse at New York Fashion Week, 1987.

THE GREAT FASHION SHOWMAN

TENTH ANNIVERSARY COLLECTION
THIERRY MUGLER
1984

To celebrate the tenth anniversary of his label in March 1984, Thierry Mugler pulled out the stops with a $1 million dollar show for his fall–winter 1984–1985 collection, presented to a 6,000-strong audience of paying guests and the press.

Held at the Zénith Paris stadium, it was the first mass commerical fashion show, and much like in an elaborate pop concert, the French designer created a series of vignettes, including Olympian, Space Age and religious motifs. Three hundred and fifty outfits were shown to the audience, and with a theme of exalted beauty, the models were given halos and angel wings. In one spectacular moment, the model Pat Cleveland, who was six months pregnant, was dressed as the Virgin Mary. In a transparent blue chiffon gown, with a harness attached to her, she descended from the ceilings bathed in smoke, as if coming from the heavens. It was a show-stopping vision that raised fashion to a religious experience and was controversial in its use of a pregnant model in a divine depiction, at a time when prenatal women were expected to retreat from the public. The celestial moment was described by journalist Marion Hume as 'a brave, deranged declaration that fashion designers, and even ordinary mortals, need not be confined by the gravity of planet Earth'.

Throughout the 1980s, Mugler celebrated an exalted, flawless female aesthetic, with his body-conscious designs on Amazonian models. His shows became elaborate productions, casting supermodels, drag queens, Hollywood actresses and porn stars – Traci Lords appeared on the runway for a 1992 Aids charity event.

Models were dressed as mermaids for the spring–summer 1989 ready-to-wear show, and for his autumn–winter 1995–1996 show, at the Cirque d'Hiver in Paris, to mark his twentieth-anniversary, he dressed his models as unreal androids.

'There are two ways you can do fashion shows today,' Mugler commented, after his spectacular 1984 show. 'Either you do it very small and private or you do this. I think the public wants it this way.'

Iman modeling for Thierry Mugler's ambitious Paris show in 1984.

THE RISE OF THE COUNTERCULTURE 1954–1984

GENERATION
X AND Y

1980–2007

The last decades of the twentieth century were marked by a new wave of mass consumption and mass media, and as fashion became excessive and expressive, it reflected societal and economic changes around the world.

In the late 1970s brands like Ralph Lauren and Calvin Klein exploded onto the scene. With the dollar going from strength to strength, there was high demand for luxury clothing and couture. Labels like Chanel, transformed under the direction of Karl Lagerfeld, Christian Lacroix and Moschino captured the desire for extravagant, gaudy glamour, as played out on popular TV shows *Dallas* and *Dynasty*, where shoulder pads were big and colours were bold and bright.

Diana, Princess of Wales, was the style icon of the decade, and she brought glamour to the royal family while promoting British designers Bruce Oldfield and Catherine Walker. It was also the era of the supermodel, where Cindy Crawford and Iman showcased a healthy, lustrous look and commanded higher-than-ever fees for their appearances. In 1989, Gianni Versace opened his atelier, and along with Dolce & Gabbana, founded in Milan in 1988, promoted a sexy, high-voltage look for the 1990s. Versace would earn huge publicity with his autumn–winter 1991 show that cast the Big Four supermodels, Cindy Crawford, Naomi Campbell, Linda Evangelista and Christy Turlington, and in 1994 when Elizabeth Hurley wore the 'safety-pin' dress to the premiere of *Four Weddings and a Funeral*.

A CHANGING LANDSCAPE

By the late 1980s, the economic bubble was bursting, and the 'greed is good' ethos had become tired. New youth movements rose up from the yuppie society, with the hedonism of rave culture marking 1988 as the new Summer of Love. By the early 1990s, a burgeoning subculture that was the antithesis of 1980s overload also emerged from the rainy Pacific Northwest. The grunge mentality was anti-fashion, throwing together thrift store finds and cheap pieces from the bottom of a bargain bin, as represented by bands like Nirvana and Pearl Jam.

Kate Moss became the face of a new form of beauty following her appearance in advertisements for Calvin Klein jeans, underwear and fragrance. She would become representative of the grunge movement, of the controversial Heroin Chic look of fashion photography and the muse of a new generation of hot designers like Marc Jacobs and Alexander McQueen.

It was Tom Ford who brought a sense of glamour back to the 1990s, following the wave of anti-fashion movements. As the creative director of Gucci, in 1995, he launched a sleek, minimalist and sexy style and resurrected the Gucci logo, which he would use to controversial effect in a series of risqué advertising campaigns.

THE POWER OF THE INTERNET

By the Millennium, fashion was again undergoing a reinvention through new ways of looking at design and the rise in e-commerce through the growing autonomy of the internet. Powerful new suppliers like ASOS helped push a desire for cheap, disposable clothing, while replicating the look of It girls like Sienna Miller, Paris Hilton and Misha Barton, whose paparazzi images were splashed across gossip magazines. The noughties was a period of conspicuous consumption, with a constant rotation of must-have pieces, from the latest It bag to the hot mobile phone accessory, as sought after by Generation Y, the first group of young people brought up on the internet.

'THE EARLY 1990S WERE AN ESPECIALLY MARVELLOUS PERIOD FOR FASHION, BECAUSE IT WAS THE PEAK OF GLAMOUR AND THERE WERE NO LIMITS AS TO WHAT YOU COULD DO.'

DONATELLA VERSACE

1980
→ Calvin Klein launches his line of jeans, with a controversial series of adverts starring Brooke Shields.

1981
→ Comme des Garçons, the Japanese label founded by Rei Kawakubo and Yohji Yamamoto, shows in Paris for the first time.
→ Ronald Reagan is inaugurated as President of the United States of America.
→ Lady Diana Spencer marries Prince Charles at St Paul's Cathedral, London, wearing a wedding gown partly influenced by the New Romantics.
→ New Wave band Blondie release their single 'Rapture', featuring a rap by Debbie Harry.

1984
→ Record label Def Jam is founded, going on to launch some of the most influential hip-hop bands.

1986
→ Run DMC release their ode to the sneaker, 'My Adidas'.

1987
→ The US stock market crash known as Black Monday marks the start of a period of recession.

1988
→ Anna Wintour is appointed editor-in-chief at American *Vogue*.

1989
→ Gianni Versace opens his fashion house.
→ Miuccia Prada revives the Prada brand when she launches its first ready-to-wear collection.

1990
→ Sixteen-year-old Kate Moss appears on the cover of *The Face* magazine with the headline 'The Third Summer of Love'.
→ Madonna's Blond Ambition tour revolutionizes the theatricality of pop and sparks controversy with her Jean Paul Gaultier conical corsets.

1991
→ Seattle band Nirvana's second studio album *Nevermind* is released, bringing grunge to a mainstream audience.

1993

→ Marc Jacobs releases his grunge collection for Perry Ellis.

→ Japanese designer Issey Miyake launches his first Pleats Please collection.

→ Alexander McQueen holds his first runway show; spring–summer 1994's Nihilism collection.

1994

→ Gucci appoints Tom Ford as creative director to introduce sex appeal.

→ Elizabeth Hurley hits the headlines, wearing a Versace safety-pin dress to the *Four Weddings and a Funeral* premiere.

1995

→ The Wu-Tang Clan launch their Wu Wear clothing label.

1996

→ The Spice Girls release their debut single 'Wannabe'.

1997

→ Oasis's Liam Gallagher and Patsy Kensit appear on the cover of *Vanity Fair* on a Union Jack sheet, marking the peak of Brit Pop.

→ Photographer Shoichi Aoki launches *FRUiTS* magazine, capturing unique Tokyo street style.

2001

→ Stella McCartney launches her own label, and will go on to earn a reputation for her environmental awareness.

→ Burberry appoints Christopher Bailey as creative director to reposition it as a luxury brand.

2005

→ Kate Moss redefines boho festival chic when she appears at Glastonbury in a waistcoat, hot pants and wellington boots.

2007

→ The start of the Great Recession, which lasts until 2009.

SUPERSTAR SNEAKERS

RUN DMC COLLABORATION
ADIDAS
1986

In May 1986, when Run DMC released their single 'My Adidas' as an ode to their favourite footwear, it almost immediately set a blueprint for the way sportswear advertising would collide with music. When the band started asking audiences to hold up their sneakers during the anthem, Adidas realised the power of the group's influence and gave them an offer they couldn't refuse: they received the first ever non-sports endorsement by a sportswear brand.

Adidas was founded in Bavaria in 1924 by twenty-four-year-old Adi Dassler, but it wasn't until after World War II that he registered his business and developed the signature three stripes for which the brand is known. As sportswear took off in the 1970s, Adidas competed with other brands like Reebok, Puma and Nike, which were all trying to get their own foothold in the industry.

As part of hip-hop culture, 'being fresh' was vital, and out-of-the-box trainers were an essential component to the style. Run DMC was a hip-hop group that crossed into the rock scene with their guitar riffs and leathers, and the Brooklyn trio had worn Adidas trainers without laces as a reference to the way inmates were stripped of them to prevent them from hanging themselves.

As they toured across the United States, the band observed audiences copying their tracksuits, gold chains and white sneakers, and so they put together 'My Adidas' as a shout-out to fans. During performances of the song, the crowds would hold up their own sneakers in mass tribute.

'I wear my Adidas when I rock the beat,' they rapped. When Adidas executive Angelo Anastasio saw this moment at Madison Square Gardens, he offered up a record 1 million dollars for Run DMC to be the face of the brand – an unprecedented amount for any musician or band.

Their association led to half a million pairs of Adidas being sold that same year, and the brand further collaborated on a Run DMC sneaker, along with sweatshirts and signature leather tracksuits.

The sportswear and hip-hop collaboration opened up further deals and fashion started to ride on the back of hip-hop's enormous reach. By the 1990s and 2000s, it had exploded into a billion-dollar industry, where sports and fashion brands like Ralph Lauren and Tommy Hilfiger tried to capitalize on their reputation as sought after labels by hip-hop bands and the teenage fans who copied them.

Run DMC in New York, 1985.

GENERATION X AND Y 1980–2007

HIP-HOP FASHION

In the early 1970s, the South Bronx was a place of poverty and unemployment and home to youth gangs like Savage Skulls and Black Spades. It was here that hip-hop was founded; a subculture that would become a billion-dollar business incorporating fashion and music as an expression of the African-American experience. The movement was not only concerned with Black pride and empowerment, but was about creativity through four elements – MCing, DJing, graffiti and breakdancing.

Block parties sprung up around the Bronx in the early 1970s, and at every party the breakdancers, or b-boys, would show off their considerable moves, developing a crisp new sportswear style which focused on being 'fresh'. Their look, which featured pristine shell-toe Adidas Superstar sneakers with straight-legged Lee jeans, velour tracksuits with same-brand trainers and Kangol Bermuda hats, went global when real-life breakdancers appeared in the 1984 movie *Wild Style*, featuring elements of hip-hop.

While the East Coast developed the original hip-hop style, Los Angeles brought 'gangsta rap' to public consciousness, with Compton's NWA and Ice-T shocking America with their violent depictions of police brutality and social issues in the Black community. Compton style became the pervading image of hip-hop. Trousers were worn low, without a belt, as a reference to prisoners having their belts removed in jail, and sweatshirts were accessorised with large chains around the neck. As hip-hop stars gained success and money, the concept of 'bling' would become part of the fashion industry. It displayed the wealth accumulated from escaping the ghetto with gold 'grillz' on the teeth and outlandish, excessive medallions embellished with diamonds.

Designer labels were always a part of the aspirational side of hip-hop, with Ralph Lauren and Tommy Hilfiger worshipped by street gangs who appropriated middle-class American labels to create new meaning. In 1989, Carl Williams became the first African-American to launch a hip-hop fashion line with his label Karl Kani, and by the mid-1990s hip-hop

(L-R) Bobcat, Cut Creator, LL Cool J, and E-Love in New York, 1987.

fashion exploded as musicians launched their own labels. While hip-hop stars had once been considered outsiders, forming their own sense of self-expression, they became part of mainstream fashion. The style was appropriated by traditional designers, and a new generation of hip-hop stars, like ASAP Rocky, advertised for Dior Homme and Calvin Klein.

As Sacha Jenkins, director of the documentary *Fresh Dressed*, commented: 'Fashion has always been an important part of the hip-hop identity because fashion has always been an important part of black identity in America. Because when you don't have much ownership over where you can land in society, your financial situation, your educational situation, the one thing you can control is the way you look.'

CONFRONTATIONAL SEXUALITY

MADONNA'S CONICAL CORSETS
JEAN PAUL GAULTIER
1990

Madonna's Blond Ambition tour kicked off in April 1990 in Chiba, Japan, where the pop star launched an explosive spectacle that told the story of her career through Catholic imagery with risqué choreography, BDSM, art deco and German Expressionism themes. It was the first time a major pop concert fused music, dance and the theatrical, and the Jean Paul Gaultier-designed costumes of exaggerated corsets and conical bras worn with pin-striped suits or fishnet tights, helped to elevate Madonna, and the corsets, to cultural icon status.

The sexual imagery of the tour, of Madonna with phallic-like bra cups, masturbating on a plush velvet bed while performing 'Like a Virgin', caused a huge backlash around the world. In Toronto, the police threatened her with arrest if she didn't cancel her show. In Italy, Pope John Paul II declared her concert 'one of the most satanic shows in the history of humanity'.

Jean Paul Gaultier's designs for the show built on earlier innovations from his collections. He first showcased phallic conical bras, like whipped ice-cream cones, for an orange velvet dress in his autumn–winter 1984–1985 collection, Barbès. The style was inspired by the bullet bras of the 1950s, which gave women a lethal shape under their tight sweaters, and in the September 1984 issue of British *Vogue*, a review described them as 'Just two cornetti from Gaultier'.

The conical corsets were pieces of craftsmanship with luxury satin fabric and exquisite lacing, and which referenced Horst's famous photograph of Mainbocher's corset in 1939 (see pages 48–49). They were also subversive in the way they redefined the female body. Rather than a soft shape, they showed Madonna's muscular body with exaggerated, spiky cones for breasts, described by one critic as a Freudian nightmare. As Madonna said: 'They're pointed. So there's something slightly dangerous about them. If you bump into them, you'll cut yourself.'

The costumes for Blond Ambition demonstrated Madonna's dominance and power, reaffirming her position as the Queen of Pop. The corsets also left a legacy in their influence on the stage costumes of other pop stars, from Kylie Minogue to Lady Gaga, and would be endlessly referenced and parodied, in sketches by French and Saunders and in the countless imitations found in costume stores. But Madonna's collaboration with Jean Paul Gaultier remains a template for erotically charged statements on gender, sexuality and personal freedom of expression. In Gaultier's words, 'A tough outer shell at times protects hidden vulnerability.'

Madonna performing her Blond Ambition tour in Rotterdam, 1990.

GENERATION X AND Y 1980—2007

THE NEW WAIF-LIKE MINIMALISM

CALVIN KLEIN ADVERTS
KATE MOSS
1992

Calvin Klein may have built up his empire in the 1980s from his controversial jeans commercials featuring a teenage Brooke Shields, but by the 1990s his business was on the verge of bankruptcy. He was in desperate need of finding a way to revitalise his brand by tapping into the youthful demographic to sell his jeans, T-shirts and underwear line.

In the early 1990s, the excesses of the previous decade had been swept away by a new generation concerned by the AIDS crisis and unemployment; they favoured grit over glam. Klein consulted with his switched-on team to uncover the latest trends, and they sensed that the photos taken by Corinne Day of Kate Moss, a waifish young model with jagged teeth, which had appeared in hip UK magazine *The Face*, conveyed the realism that was very much of that moment. The one image Klein focused on was a black-and-white shot taken in July 1990, featuring Moss with a wide smile and her freckles clearly visible. On the back of this photo, eighteen-year-old Moss was hired by Calvin Klein to invigorate the brand, as she could pull off the minimalist look of jeans and T-shirts needed to appeal to an audience of young people. As Maureen Callahan wrote in her book *Champagne Supernovas*, 'this meant going younger, less crisp and arch – almost dirtier'.

Starring alongside Moss in the initial photoshoot by Herb Ritz was Mark Wahlberg, then known as hip-hop performer Marky Mark, and famous for his bad-boy attitude and his gym-honed abs. He was the beefcake and she was the waif, and Moss found being topless on the shoot uncomfortable as Wahlberg was rude and disinterested. She later confessed that the photoshoot had been traumatising, and she had felt 'really bad about straddling this buff guy. I didn't like it. I couldn't get out of bed for two weeks.'

As soon as the campaign was launched, it reignited interest in the Calvin Klein brand, affording the opportunity to open a vast 20,000 foot flagship store on New York's Madison Avenue in 1995. The ads also firmly established Moss as the star. Wahlberg was dropped from the campaign and she became the sole face of Calvin Klein jeans, underwear and perfume, always shot in black and white, sometimes topless or wearing a simple tank top, with little make-up. The messaging in these adverts, like those of Brooke Shields over ten years before, was that sex most definitely sells.

While the mass advertising campaigns boosted sales among teenagers, Moss and Klein were also heavily criticized in the press. Klein had already been accused of child pornography with his 1980 campaign featuring fifteen-year old Brooke

Mark Wahlberg and Kate Moss in Calvin Klein's 1992 advert.

Shields, breathing 'You know what comes between me and my Calvins? Nothing', and this time he was lambasted for promoting what became known as the Heroin Chic look.

While Kate Moss was at first credited with having a more down-to-earth, relatable appeal than the unattainable beauty of supermodels like Cindy Crawford and Claudia Schiffer, she was also maligned in the press for appearing underfed. Her thin frame raised concerns for presenting an unhealthy body image to teenage girls and thus promoting anorexia. In New York, there were reports of billboards of Moss being defaced with the words: 'Feed Me. Please send breadcrumbs c/o Calvin Klein.'

Despite the barrage of abuse that her body was too thin, as a result of the campaign, Kate Moss quickly reached stratospheric levels of fame, and Calvin Klein would follow up with another groundbreaking, minimalist campaign for CK One, reflecting the grittier style that had been inspired by Moss.

'I WANTED SOMEONE WHO WAS NATURAL, ALWAYS THIN. I WAS LOOKING FOR THE COMPLETE OPPOSITE OF THAT GLAMOUR TYPE THAT CAME BEFORE KATE.'

CALVIN KLEIN

Linda, Cindy, Naomi and Christy at Versace's 1991 show.

In 1989, Herb Ritz took a black-and-white photo for *Rolling Stone* that featured the highest-paid models of the time, Cindy Crawford, Naomi Campbell, Christy Turlington, Stephanie Seymour and Tatjana Patitz, with their nude bodies entwined. It placed them firmly as celebrity icons, going beyond the world of fashion by discarding their clothes for a music magazine, and helping to launch the term 'supermodel'. These women held such extraordinary power that their names had more prestige than the brands they modelled for.

When they appeared on the runway for Versace's 1991 show, Naomi Campbell, Cindy Crawford, Linda Evangelista and Christy Turlington redefined the word 'model'. Their glossy, Amazonian appeal represented not just the excesses of Gianni Versace's designs but also the consumerism and glamour of the era. That moment ushered in a period of dominance for supermodels, as Linda Evangelista evinced when she declared, 'I won't get out of bed for less than $10,000 a day.' They branched out into workout videos, acting, presenting roles and cosmetic lines.

Later they were known as the Big Six, when Claudia Schiffer and Kate Moss joined their ranks. Moss had her own unique look as the grunge model who would also come to represent the contentious Heroin Chic. While a new breed of supermodels, many made famous by the Victoria's Secret fashion shows, found fame from the late 1990s, it was the original supermodels who retained their legendary status for their untouchable presence and glamour.

GRUNGE DELUXE

GRUNGE COLLECTION
MARC JACOBS FOR PERRY ELLIS
1993

In 1992, grunge was everywhere. Nirvana, Sound Garden and Pearl Jam were playing on radio stations around the world, the antics of Kurt Cobain and Courtney Love generated headlines, and Winona Ryder and Johnny Depp, in their ripped jeans and leathers, were snapped by paparazzi. It seemed like Seattle, the birthplace of grunge, was now the hippest city on the planet. Almost every teenager on the street was copying their favourite musicians on MTV by dressing in flannel shirts, with their baggy sweaters tied around their waists. Grunge was very much of the moment, and twenty-nine year-old Marc Jacobs, designer at Perry Ellis and looking to elevate the brand following the death of its founder from AIDS seven years before, was inspired to translate this street style into his next collection.

As he planned out the concept for his spring 1993 ready-to-wear collection, he thought of the hip actresses like Juliette Lewis, Drew Barrymore and Julia Roberts, who dressed as if they'd bought their clothes from charity shops, and he created a mood board with images of Kate Moss by Corinne Day from *The Face*. Jacobs took cheap flannel shirts and wool caps from thrift stores, sending them to Italy to remake them in expensive silk and cashmere, and commissioned Birkenstock and Converse to make versions of their shoes in duchess satin. It was a luxury interpretation of a movement that, at its heart, was considered 'anti-fashion', and which Jacobs himself described as a 'hippied romantic version of punk'.

By the time the collection was ready to launch, grunge was going mainstream, and with the release of Cameron Crowe's Generation X movie *Singles*, the ubiquity of grunge bands in the charts and Courtney Love featuring on the cover of *Vanity Fair* in September 1992, it was beginning to become a little passé. When Jacobs sent models like Christy Turlington, Carla Bruni, Helena Christensen and Kate Moss down the catwalk in beany hats, floaty dresses and combat boots, he thought it would make his name, but instead of praise, Jacobs was ridiculed by the fashion press.

Anna Wintour of *Vogue* was the only editor to see the potential, featuring Kristen McMenamy and Naomi Campbell in a ten-page spread, with photos by Steven Meisel. But for others, Jacobs' show provoked strong feelings. Fashion critic Suzy Menkes of the *International Herald Tribune* detested it so much that she had 'Grunge Is Ghastly' badges created. Faced with this onslaught, Jacobs was fired by Perry Ellis. *The New York Times* joined in with the criticism, with Rick Marin describing Jacobs' final runway show for Perry Ellis as a mess. 'The

Model Christy Turlington walks Perry Ellis' spring-summer 1993 RTW Runway collection

music—by the alternative bands Sonic Youth, Nirvana, and L7—was loud, aggressive, and to some, overbearing ... One model even wore a nose ring.' The newspaper also ridiculed how the 'flannel' shirt which models had tied around their waists was 'sand-washed silk'. *New York* magazine further announced 'Grunge: 1992–1993, RIP'.

For many, Jacobs' collection represented the final shove that killed off a street movement. Ultimately, Jacobs proved them wrong. After recovering from the humiliation, he launched a label under his own name, which quickly earned a reputation as a favourite of cool 'boho' girls like Kate Moss, Chloë Sevigny and Sienna Miller. Twenty-six years later, he reissued twenty-six pieces from the collection, naming it Grunge Redux and hiring some of the original models like Kristen McMenamy and her daughter, Lily, to model the clothes. It was his way of demonstrating that his grunge vision had a long-lasting legacy.

In 1993, however, the final nail in the coffin was a photo of Kurt Cobain in a black T-shirt that read 'Grunge Is Dead', while holding his baby daughter, Frances Bean. Courtney Love further cemented the boredom with the movement: 'Marc sent me and Kurt his Perry Ellis grunge collection. Do you know what we did with it? We burned it.'

'MARC SENT ME AND KURT HIS PERRY ELLIS GRUNGE COLLECTION. DO YOU KNOW WHAT WE DID WITH IT? WE BURNED IT.'

COURTNEY LOVE

While the early 1990s was considered the era of the supermodel, Kate Moss rose to fame through the grungy, cool images taken by Corinne Day for *The Face* magazine. Day's images of Moss's waifish, almost skeletal body launched what was to become known as Heroin Chic. Other models who were representative of the aesthetic included Jaime King and Jodie Kidd, whose frames would be criticised for being unhealthily thin, and Gia Carangi, whose AIDS-related death in 1986 was linked to her drug addiction. The trend coincided with the depiction of heroin use in cult films like *Kids* (1995) and *Trainspotting* (1996), and the knowledge that drugs were prevalent within the fashion industry.

The late fashion photographer Davide Sorrenti was one of the most prominent and controversial figures at the forefront of this style. He captured models with thin bodies, stringy hair, pale skin and dark circles under their eyes, as if they were living off cigarettes, coffee and drugs. Sorrenti's raw images gained notoriety when he was accused of encouraging eating disorders, drug abuse and chain-smoking. Among those condemning it and its influence was President Bill Clinton, who said 'The glorification of heroin' was 'destructive'.

When Sorrenti tragically died in 1997 from an overdose, it brought to an end the Heroin Chic trend. It marked a new era for the supermodel aesthetic as promoted by Gisele Bündchen and Victoria's Secret angels like Adriana Lima; an aesthetic that would later be criticised for promoting an unobtainable notion of female beauty.

THE NEW EROGENOUS ZONE

THE BUMSTER
ALEXANDER MCQUEEN
1993

Lee Alexander McQueen smashed his way into fashion with his first collection, Taxi Driver, inspired by the Martin Scorcese film. It was a modest start for the *enfant terrible* of the fashion world, but there was one look from his collection that would create shockwaves: the bumster.

McQueen was a fashion vanguard with a punk aesthetic, using his vision to provoke the fashion establishment and to confront his audience with uncomfortable subjects. 'I want people to fear the women I dress,' he said. After graduating from Central Saint Martins, he was one of six young British designers chosen to have their work shown during London's Fashion Week in 1993 at hotel rooms in the Ritz. His patron, Isabella Blow, acted as his PR person, pulling people into McQueen's room to take a look at the collection hanging on a rail, including his bumsters. These tailored trousers were slim-fitting and worn so low that they revealed a section of the buttocks, effectively changing the shape of the body.

For McQueen's first runway show, his spring–summer 1994 collection entitled Nihilism, the bumster was back with a vengeance, with models painted with bruises and blood, and with their extreme low-rise jeans showing the cracks of their buttocks. Marion Hume in *The Independent*, on 21 October 1993, described feeling 'queasy' but stayed in her seat to witness the 'catalogue of horrors' because the designer had something new to say, about 'battered women, of violent lives, of grinding daily existences offset by wild, drug-enhanced nocturnal dives into clubs where the dress code is semi-naked'. She also praised his 'daringly new trousers'.

For his next collection, the spring–summer 1995 The Birds collection, he repurposed the bumster as skin-tight, luxe pencil-skirts for Hitchcock heroines, and for his autumn–winter 1995 Highland Rape collection, he created a 'bumster' black silk taffeta skirt. For his autumn–winter 1996 Dante collection, models like Kate Moss wore acid-wash denim versions, for deconstructed, violent sex appeal.

From its conception, the bumster was an immediate conversation starter. It was ridiculed in the mainstream press but celebrated by fashionistas and, in 1994 when she wore a pair of bumsters for an advert on MTV, Madonna helped to bring the style into the mainstream. A decade later, McQueen's influence was still evident, with the Sunday Independent in August 2004 commenting that since he launched the butt cleavage of the bumster, 'low-rise jeans have been the bane of most women's lives'!

Alexander McQueen's autumn–winter 1996 'Dante' collection at New York Fashion Week.

GENERATION X AND Y 1980–2007

PERMANENT PLEATS

FLYING SAUCER DRESS
ISSEY MIYAKE
1994

Opening up like a concertina, with ice-lolly stripes, Issey Miyake's Flying
Saucer dress brought fresh new innovation to the catwalk when he showcased
it at his spring–summer 1994 collection. Taking its shape from a paper lantern,
the tubular polyester dress could be pulled on like a slinky toy, with the shape
changing to fit the body underneath. Once taken off, it returned to its folded
shape for easy storage.

The Flying Saucer dress was part of the Japanese designer's Pleats Please
collection, where each garment was constructed from just one piece of 100 per
cent polyester fabric and fed into a heat press to create permanent pleats. It was
easy to wear and could be flattened for packing, didn't require ironing and was
also sustainable – an interest of Miyake's long before the rest of the fashion
industry caught on.

After studying graphic design in Tokyo, Miyake arrived in Paris in 1965, where
he studied fashion and worked under Hubert de Givenchy. Having witnessed the
student riots of 1967, and rather than dress the bourgeoisie, he chose to create
practical, innovative clothing that was accessible. He opened the Miyake Design
Studio in 1970 and showed his first collection in New York in 1971.

Miyake first launched his pleats line in 1988, using new fabric technology to
create vertical, horizontal and zig-zag pleating, and by the time of his spring–
summer 1994 collection, he developed it as a brand in its own right. The Flying
Saucer dress created new possibilities for functional clothing. As the designer's
garments were almost weightless, they could be flattened and extended, and they
were incredibly comfortable to wear as they moved with the body.

For autumn–winter 1994, Miyake further continued to showcase his pleats,
combining shimmering dresses with innovative hats, some made from pasta and
bread or from black plastic bags. This added to the sense of deconstruction and
recycling in his designs. 'His collections are always filled with whimsy and charm,
but this time Issey Miyake has surpassed himself,' wrote Bernadine Morris in *The
New York Times* in March 1994.

The Pleats Please garments were sold from Miyake's own Pleats Please
shops, first opened in New York in 1998, to supply affordable pleated garments in
a variety of colours and styles. In 2016, *The Observer* stated: 'They are light,
ageless, trans-seasonal, cross-cultural, ambisexual … and don't cost a fortune.'

Pleats Please dresses at Issey Miyake's spring–summer 1995 show.

FROM SAFETY-PIN TO INSTANT FAME

SAFETY-PIN DRESS
VERSACE
1994

It took one dramatic Versace dress to catapult Elizabeth Hurley, a little-known actress and model, to instant fame. In May 1994, she accompanied boyfriend Hugh Grant, star of Richard Curtis' new rom-com, *Four Weddings and a Funeral*, to the premiere. By wearing the cleavage-enhancing, leg-revealing black gown, held together with safety-pins, she was the paparazzi dream of the night, ensuring that she was the only one anyone was talking about.

Designed by Gianni Versace, the tight black gown had previously been worn by Helena Christensen in the spring–summer 1994 runway show, and it perfectly encapsulated the designer's brash, voluptuous supermodel aesthetic. Plunging to the bellybutton and slit completely up the sides, the stretchy silk and Lycra fabric was held together by twenty-four large gold safety-pins embossed with the Versace medusa head, which gave it a punk, DIY edge.

Grant later recollected that Hurley only chose to wear the dress at the last minute, when other designers wouldn't lend her anything from their collections. 'Poor Elizabeth rang some top designers and they all said: "No, who are you?" or "No, we're not lending you anything." Then Versace said: "Yes, we'll lend you a dress", and they just sent one round which is that one with the safety-pins. So she shoved it on and I raised my eyebrows a fraction and we set off.'

With a winning smile and several acres of cleavage brandished before her, Elizabeth knew she had upstaged everyone – including her dishy star boyfriend. 'You cannot wear a dress like that and underestimate its impact,' wrote the *Mirror*'s Fiona McIntosh, the day after the premiere. The newspaper also reported that the telephones at Versace's London office were running off the hook with requests for the 'pin dress', but by that time the $2,580 dress was sold out. Hurley not only became one of the hottest celebrities in the world, despite only a few film credits under her belt, but Versace quickly became a household name for its lustrous fashion excesses.

From then on simply referred as 'That Dress', it would became a symbol of immediate celebrity, where all someone needed to grab the attention of the press was a voluptuous body and a revealing gown. Hurley paved the way for actresses like Rose McGowan, wearing sheer mesh and just a thong underneath, and Jennifer Lopez in a split-to-the-navel Versace gown, to reach next levels of fame.

Elizabeth Hurley and Hugh Grant at the May 1994 *Four Weddings and a Funeral* premiere.

PLATFORM TRAINERS FOR GIRL POWER

BUFFALO TRAINERS
SPICE GIRLS
1996

Buffalo's boots and trainers, with their stacked platform heels, gained huge momentum in the mid-1990s, particularly after the British supergroup the Spice Girls high-kicked their way into pop culture.

When the girl group's debut single 'Wannabe' was released on 8 July 1996, it spent seven weeks at number one in the UK and four in the US, and made overnight stars of its five members, Scary Spice (Mel B/Melanie Brown), Sporty Spice (Mel C/Melanie Chisholm), Posh Spice (then Victoria Adams now Beckham), Baby Spice (Emma Bunton) and Ginger Spice (Geri Halliwell).

The Spice Girls could be bubble-gum sweet, fizzy as pop and loud and confrontational, and they each defined their own image, making them even more accessible to their fans. They promoted girl power, of being who you want to be, and they chose to wear their Buffalo trainers in music videos and on photoshoots to enhance their image of freedom and fun. There was nothing soft and feminine about the shoes – while they boosted the height by five inches, they weren't delicate, rather were clompy, but they fitted the aesthetics and attitude of the ladette culture of the mid-1990s, where girls were unapologetic in their clothing.

Buffalo, founded in Frankfurt in 1979, originally manufactured cowboy boots, but in 1995 they created a line of boots with platform soles which became known as the Buffalo Classic. The leather boots and sneakers with colossal soles had become a cult favourite for ravers in clubs and fields across Britain, before hitting the fashion press when sported by the Spice Girls. Scary Spice wore hers in leopard print, Baby Spice in candy colours, Sporty Spice teamed hers with tracksuits and Ginger Spice wore red leather platforms with her Union Jack mini-dress at the 1997 Brit Awards. It was only Posh Spice, known for her little black dresses, who was too sophisticated to wear a pair.

While Buffalo boots created a buzz, there were also stories in the press about their hazardous nature. After she tripped on a TV show in Turkey in 1997, Emma Bunton was forced to deny rumours that her Buffalo boots were the cause of her sprained ankle. Not since Naomi Campbell took a tumble in sky-high Vivienne Westwood shoes had footwear been considered so dangerous or subversive.

The Spice Girls at the 1997 MTV Video Music Awards in New York.

GENERATION X AND Y 1980–2007

THE UGLY IDEA OF BEAUTY

BANAL ECCENTRICITY
PRADA
1996

In 1978, when Miuccia Prada inherited the luxury goods brand founded by her grandfather, she sought to disrupt fashion by hijacking 'the codes of the upper bourgeoisie'. In 1984, she introduced the hugely successful nylon backpack, inverting what was considered luxury at the time, and in 1988 she launched Prada's first womenswear collection. This desire to dress women in ways that played against conventions, with mismatched colours, prints and style, was fully embraced in her spring–summer 1996 collection.

While previous collections had featured minimal black and floral prints, Prada found that by taking the clashing, unflattering styles of a 1970s librarian, she tapped into a youth culture moment in the mid-1990s. It was defined by dressing in ways that confounded beauty expectations, choosing to underplay sexiness by wearing clothes that would be considered passé. Adding a touch of something that was thought to be 'bad taste' became the ultimate in chic, partly triggered by the Britpop phenomenon that marked the middle of the decade.

With the smash success of their single 'Common People' in 1995, British indie band Pulp made an indelible impact on pop culture and on how bands were expected to dress. Frontman Jarvis Cocker and the other five members triggered a trend for a 1970s revival of charity-shop sweaters, knitted tank tops and thick-rimmed glasses, as they adopted a style that was more geography teacher than rock star. Their look was given a name, 'geek chic', and the clashing prints and jumble-shop aesthetic was brought to the catwalk for Prada's spring–summer 1996 collection, where what was 'uncool' quickly became cool.

Prada's show, officially named Banal Eccentricity, but dubbed Ugly Chic, dressed models Kate Moss and Amber Valetta in a 1970s silhouette of A-line skirts and wide-lapelled shirts, with geometric patterns mixing clashing shades of muddy brown, citron, aubergine and rust. Just like Pulp and other Britpop musicians, the look was a mish-mash of different styles. Despite the dowdiness of the skirts, worn with chunky heels, it was a refreshing alternative to the obviously sexy glamour of Tom Ford's designs for Gucci. It was, in the words of Amy Spindler of *The New York Times*, 'A timely tribute to a younger generation that has a new sense of color, and an older generation that lived through such bizarre mixes in the 1970s.'

The collection caused a sensation for its radical twist on what was considered chic. 'Ugly is in,' wrote Robin D. Givhan in *The Washington Post* in May 1996. She described how the silhouette was 'stiff and unflattering' and the colours 'hovered somewhere between shades of slime and mold. The browns

Prada's spring–summer 1996 show, Banal Eccentricity.

GENERATION X AND Y 1980–2007

were murky – the color of water as it stagnates over a long, steamy summer.' In *Vogue*, Plum Sykes praised the collection, and described how suddenly 'ordinariness and bad taste seem refreshing'.

For Miuccia Prada, the fine line between bad taste and chic elegance was something worth exploring in detail. 'The investigation of ugliness is, to me, more interesting than the bourgeois idea of beauty. And why? Because ugly is human. It touches the bad and the dirty side of people,' she said. '... It was not used in fashion and I was very much criticised for inventing the trashy and the ugly.'

The collection would have an impact on how people wore patterns and colours for the next few years. Bold wallpaper-like prints filtered into the high street, and there was a widespread trend for mixing contemporary fashion with second-hand and charity-shop finds. Alexander Fury wrote in *The Independent* that the Prada Ugly Chic collection 'got us all to wear chocolate brown and gave vintage sales a boost. In retrospect, it caused a seismic sartorial shift in a similar manner to Christian Dior's "New Look" of 1947.'

'THE INVESTIGATION OF UGLINESS IS, TO ME, MORE INTERESTING THAN THE BOURGEOIS IDEA OF BEAUTY. AND WHY? BECAUSE UGLY IS HUMAN.'

MIUCCIA PRADA

Kate Moss in a
Clements Ribeiro
Union Jack jumper,
1998.

When celebrity couple Patsy Kensit and Liam Gallagher featured
on the cover of *Vanity Fair* in 1997, lying on a bed with a Union
Jack sheet with the headline 'London Swings Again!', it
represented the pinnacle of 'Cool Britannia' optimism.

Bands like Blur, Oasis and Pulp played to the ordinariness
of British life, with lyrics casting a cynical, comical take on the
banalities of drinking cider in the park, coming up on an E in a
field and first-time sex. Their clothing reflected this ordinariness,
with a football casual style that combined with the 1960s mod
look and a tomboy aesthetic for girls. It sparked trends for Adidas
trainers and Parka jackets. Clements Ribeiro launched a Union
Jack jumper modelled by Kate Moss at the height of Britpop
fever in 1997, and Ginger Spice appeared in her Union Jack
dress at the Brits.

Britpop also reflected a change in the mood of the country.
After eighteen years of a Conservative government, New Labour,
backed by Britpop stars, was voted into power in May 1997,
bringing with it a short-lived sense of hope.

LUMPS AND BUMPS

BODY MEETS DRESS AND DRESS MEETS BODY
COMME DES GARÇONS
1997

Since she began her avant-garde label, Comme des Garçons, in 1969, Rei Kawakubo has challenged traditional concepts of beauty with her surrealist designs. For her spring–summer 1997 collection titled Body Meets Dress and Dress Meets Body, but forever referred to as Lumps and Bumps, she used padding to create the effect of tumours growing from parts of the body that were rarely accentuated.

The pretty, non-threatening fabrics, in red-and-white gingham and blue-and-white stripes, were pulled tightly over the kidney-shaped padding sewn into the linings. These created bumps that grew from the buttocks, at the neck and shoulders and around the stomach, which distorted the models' silhouettes. Rather than just walking down the catwalk, esteemed choreographer Merce Cunningham created movements to show the way the padding affected the perception of the body when seen from different angles. The collection was reminiscent of the Incroyables of the post-Revolution Directoire period of France, who used padding to imply hunchbacks, and who shortened their jackets and pulled up the collars to hide their necks for an unnerving appearance.

At a time when the Wonderbra told women they needed to enhance their cleavage with padding, and Tom Ford was sending glossy supermodels down the catwalk in thongs, Kawakubo parodied these beauty ideals with shapes that deviated from the norm. As Valerie Steele wrote, Kawakubo 'challenged the social construction of woman as the beautiful sex … No longer is fashion a false surface that seeks to create the impression of a naturally beautiful female doll. Instead, it exemplifies a new kind of embodiment.'

Fashion writer Suzy Menkes recalled the shockwaves among the audience viewing the show, which caused 'a feeling of alarm and being scared and being worried because of these extraordinary changes of shape … it was a moment when we felt we were being shown something more than clothes.'

While the collection received some praise from the press, fashion magazines like *Vogue* and *Elle* decided to feature the clothes with the padding removed. 'I didn't expect them to be easy garments to be worn everyday,' Kawakubo said of her collection. 'It is more important, I think, to translate thought into action rather than to worry about if one's clothes are worn in the end. This is probably why the collection stimulated strong feelings in many people.'

Comme des Garçons' spring–summer 1997 collection, nicknamed 'Lumps and Bumps'.

UNIQUE AND FRUITY STREET STYLE

FRUiTS MAGAZINE
SHOICHI AOKI
1997

The unique and eccentric street style found in Tokyo's Harajuku district became a worldwide phenomenon when photographer Shoichi Aoki captured the self-expression of stylish Japanese youths in a monthly magazine called *FRUiTS*, first printed in 1997.

From the late 1970s, Harajuku was the place for teenagers to gather when two of the streets were closed to traffic on Sundays. These fashion-conscious teenagers began wearing clothes that were increasingly outrageous. They were captured by Shiochi Aoki from 1997 for his magazine *FRUiTS*, the successor to an earlier publication *STREET*, which focused on overseas street style.

'Japanese street fashion has been traditionally stuff that people got from Europe and America,' said Shoichi Aoki. 'But about a year before I actually started *FRUiTS*, suddenly there was this change. People started wearing clothes that weren't influenced by the West and that prompted me to start *FRUiTS*.'

One of the most pervasive trends was for decora, meaning 'decoration', and which involved wearing unique combinations of saccharine colours and patterns, with cute, or 'kawaii', motifs. The Lolitas dressed in a sweet, Victorian style with Alice in Wonderland dresses, long socks and Mary Jane shoes from brands like Baby, The Stars Shine Bright and Alice and the Pirates, while Gothic Lolitas were influenced by the flamboyant gothic costumes worn by popular Japanese visual kei bands in the mid-1990s. They defined their own concepts of what fashion meant to them, and how they could express their personality through their distinctive, and often insane, sense of style.

Following the popularity of *FRUiTS*, Harajuku style began receiving international attention, thanks to an increased interest in street-style photography, and with pop star Gwen Stefani indebted to the look in 2004.

In February 2017 Shoichi Aoki made the decision to stop publishing *FRUiTS*, because he found that the there were fewer fashionable teenagers on the streets of Harajuku due to the rise of fast fashion.

FRUiTS didn't just open up Harajuku street fashion to global dissemination, but it would be the precursor for the popular street-style features in magazines and newspapers, where photographers would snap someone on the street and print their name, age and what they were wearing. It not only captured what was happening on ground level before it reached the catwalk, but brought fashion photography out of the mainstream, by capturing real people and real style.

FRUiTS magazine, No.13, 1998.

BJÖRK'S SWAN DRESS

BJÖRK'S ACADEMY AWARDS DRESS
MARJAN PEJOSKI
2001

Icelandic singer Björk , known for her experimental sounds and theatrical stage performances, always refused to play by the rules, and at the 2001 Academy Awards, she pushed the boundaries even further. It was the year that *Gladiator* won Best Picture, Julia Roberts won Best Actress for *Erin Brockovich* and Björk was nominated for Best Original Song, 'I've Seen It All', from Lars von Trier's *Dancing in the Dark* – a film for which she also won critical acclaim for her acting.

For some, the red carpet looks at the Oscars were more important than the ceremony itself, and the hawkish observations of critics had many stars fearful they would be put in the bad taste category. Without even considering what those reactions might be, Björk chose a feathery, life-like swan dress by Marjan Pejoski, worn over a nude bodystocking, with the head of the swan hanging limply over her shoulder. The dress was part of his autumn–winter 2001 collection and had been modelled by Alek Wek at London Fashion Week just a few weeks before.

Macedonian-born Pejoski had no idea Björk would wear his dress on the red carpet until he saw the images on the day. The concept of the eggs was Björk 's own addition, as a statement on fertility. Pejoski told *Vogue* that he laughed when he heard of it. 'It was fantastic of her. So rebellious, at a time-honoured occasion like the Oscars. I respect tradition of course, but everybody and everything deserves to be laughed at from time to time.'

As she walked down the red carpet, she caused bemusement among the other guests in their traditional Armani or Valentino, but the photographers knew that these were the shots that would command attention. As well as garnering headlines for Björk, the swan dress also became an immediate punchline for comedians. 'People didn't find it very funny,' Björk told *The New York Times* in 2007. 'They wrote about it like I was trying to wear a black Armani and got it wrong, like I was trying to fit in. Of course I wasn't trying to fit in!'

She refused to be shamed for her fashion choice, which had placed her on the worst-dressed lists, and chose to wear it on the cover of her winter-themed album *Vespertine*, as well as including it as her tour costume. Björk's risk-taking swan dress may have been contentious at the time – acerbic comedian Joan Rivers suggesting that she 'should be put into an asylum' – but she paved the way for conceptual fashions on the red carpet that came with a statement of intent.

Björk at the 2001 Academy Awards.

GENERATION X AND Y 1980—2007

HITTING THE G SPOT

GUCCI AD CAMPAIGN
TOM FORD
2003

'Sex Sells' is a mantra known well by American designer Tom Ford, and he used it to full effect as the creative director of Gucci from 1994 to 2004. When he featured an image of a model with the Gucci logo carved into her pubic hair for his spring–summer 2003 campaign, it became the most controversial of his career as he was condemned for what was described as 'deeply offensive' imagery.

When Texas-born Ford took the helm of Gucci, he was given full reign to reignite sales following a slump in profits. He introduced sleek, sexy designs displayed on gleaming models like Amber Valletta, and his runway shows became the hottest tickets for fashion editors. There were tactile velvet suits worn with teal satin shirts and clinging white dresses with erotic cut-out sections for autumn–winter 1995.

His advertising campaigns were similarly sexy. For the autumn–winter 1997 campaign, models Carolyn Murphy and Angela Lindvall embraced one another in black PVC, but the 2003 advert was the most shocking to date: the images taken by Mario Testino featured model Carmen Kass with pulled-down briefs revealing her pubic hair shaped into the G logo, while a male model kneels down beside her. It was immediately condemned by columnists like the *Daily Mail*'s Bel Mooney, damning its creators as 'no better than pimps and those who advertise sexual services in phone boxes'.

After receiving sixteen complaints, the Advertising Standards Authority in the UK launched an investigation. Gucci defended it as a 'playful' image that showed how men and women's sexual roles were changing, and that it was 'intended to be the ultimate ironic pun for a sexy brand in a logo-led age'. The ASA accepted Gucci's argument that the advert was targeted at 'modern, fashion-conscious and sophisticated adults', in fashion magazines, where it wouldn't be visible to children, and that it was 'unlikely to cause serious or widespread offence'. In comparison, Yves Saint Laurent's Opium 2000 advert featuring Sophie Dahl, nude except for a pair of heels, was banned from billboards in the UK after receiving 730 complaints, because of its visibility to children.

If Ford's aim was to generate publicity by provoking and pushing boundaries, and disrupting the fashion status quo, then the advert was one of the most successful of his career. 'Advertising campaigns became more exciting than editorial,' said Testino. 'When I started doing Gucci with Tom Ford, he pushed me to new heights.'

Gucci's controversial 2003 ad campaign.

'NO BETTER THAN PIMPS AND
THOSE WHO ADVERTISE SEXUAL
SERVICES IN PHONE BOXES.'

DAILY MAIL

RECONFIGURED SILHOUETTES

ONE HUNDRED AND ELEVEN COLLECTION
HUSSEIN CHALAYAN
2007

Described by *Vogue* as fashion's 'arch avant-gardist', and considered a magician of couture, Hussein Chalayan stunned the fashion world with his spring 2007 show, where metal animatronic dresses traversed through a century of changing silhouettes. The futuristic time-travel show, entitled One Hundred and Eleven, took the audience from 1895 to the modern day in a rapid-fire display where gowns were animated by embedded microchips.

It began with a large clock on stage, from behind which the models emerged, in a range of soft, sporty hoodies and dresses. With the sound of a ticking clock, a model walked on stage in a high-necked Victorian gown, and as she stood motionless, the clothing peeled off her and reconfigured itself. As the hemline began to rise, she was transformed into a 1920s jazz baby in a beaded flapper dress. It was followed by Dior's New Look and Paco Rabanne's metal dresses and, finally, a model stripped her clothes entirely. The show was accompanied by the sounds of those moments in time – wartime air-raids, the jet engine, clips of music.

Vogue was breathless in its praise: 'Today's spectacle was one of the increasingly rare occasions on which fashion still has the power to astonish, provoke, and send a visceral sensation through its audience. This was fashion addressing the subject of fashion, a dissection of our contemporary habit of recycling "vintage", and an embrace of high technology, all at the same time.'

Born in 1970, Chalayan and his family fled their native Cyprus following the Cypriot crisis of 1974, settling in London in 1982. As a student at Central Saint Martins, he attracted attention for his 1993 graduation collection of decomposing silk dresses that had been buried in a friend's garden. He launched his own label in 1994, and the following year, he collaborated with Björk to design her clothes for the cover of her second album *Post*, and for the tour. He was twice named British Designer of the Year in 1999 and 2000. He describes his work as telling a narrative, often drawn from his own life, of his cultural identity and migration.

Merging fashion with science, music and multimedia, Chalayan combines expert tailoring with architecture. His Geotrophics collection for spring–summer 1999 featured dresses that transformed into chairs, which represented the idea of carrying your own environment with you, and he took it even further with his 2000 collection, Afterwords. At the show held in Sadler's Well Theatre, he experimented with evolving costumes in a living-room setting, as a coffee table transformed into a skirt, and chair covers turned into dresses.

Hussein Chalayan's spring/summer 2007 ready-to-wear collection.

GENERATION X AND Y 1980–2007

His designs are symptomatic of the new Millennium, of rapidly changing technology, of a hankering for the past in the face of terrorism and political trauma, and with concerns around the damage fast fashion causes to the environment. But amid the theatrics, he creates soft, fluid clothing that don't receive as much attention as the mechanical pieces.

He has worked as creative director at sportswear brand Puma, joined the ready-to-wear creative team for Vionnet and, in 2015, opened his first store in London's Mayfair, which also served as an event space. But it's what he describes as 'scientific experiments' that receive the headlines. In his spring–summer 2016 show at Paris Fashion Week, two models stood under a shower as their water-soluble garments completely dissolved, to reveal two different designs embellished with black stitching and Swarovski crystal petals.

'The only new work you can do in fashion is via technology,' he has said. 'It lets you create something you couldn't have done in the past.'

'ONE OF THE INCREASINGLY RARE OCCASIONS ON WHICH FASHION STILL HAS THE POWER TO ASTONISH, PROVOKE, AND SEND VISCERAL SENSATION THROUGH ITS AUDIENCE.'

VOGUE

Michelle Williams, Beyoncé Knowles and Kelly Rowland of Destiny's Child.

From Paris Hilton's pink Juicy Couture tracksuits to Destiny's Child and Britney Spears' belly button-revealing outfits, noughties fashion mixed together ethnic styles with a reinvigorated girlishness and passion for pink after the ladette culture and indie bands of the 1990s.

The Millennium was marked by an explosion of new pop stars whose lifestyle and fashion were splashed across gossip magazines, as they talked on their Motorola flip-phones, sipped Starbucks iced coffees or stumbled out of a nightclub in sparkly mini-dresses. The girl fashion of the time was for hair to be worn poker straight, lips glossed, low-rise jeans, inspired by Alexander McQueen's bumster trousers, and worn with handkerchief tops and strappy shoes.

Madonna's reinvention as an Earth mother also coincided with a fashion for practicing yoga and pilates and wearing hippie styles. One of the biggest style icons was Sienna Miller, whose trademark boho-chic launched a million replica coin belts, flowing skirts and cowboy boots. Miller and model Kate Moss instigated a festival look of denim shorts, Hunter wellies or Ugg boots and they were the unfortunate pioneers of a more relentless paparazzi who recorded their every move.

Twenty years later, the Y2K style made a comeback on a wave of nostalgia for an early internet, pre-social media era with a sense of irony in re-adopting halter necks and cargo pants.

PROTEST, RESISTANCE AND SOCIAL MEDIA

2008—PRESENT

Fashion in the 2010s was shaped both by significant changes in technology, affecting the way we consume media, and by the growing sense of political energy in the air. The after-effects of the global recession of 2007 triggered a wave of discontent, which indirectly led to a fraught political climate when in 2016 Britain voted to leave the EU and Donald Trump was controversially elected President of the United States.

THE POLITICS OF FASHION

During this tumultuous decade, celebrities also became more politically charged, making a statement on the red carpet with what they chose to wear. Lady Gaga's meat dress was one of the most memorable examples, and she became infamous for the powerful statements she made through her eccentric fashion. Musicians like Beyoncé and Stormzy used their voice, and their bodies, to align with a cause. Beyoncé went down in history with her half-time Superbowl performance in 2016. She and her troupe of backing dancers paid tribute to the Black Panther movement through their black leather outfits and black berets that sent a message that Black voices wouldn't be stifled. For his 2019 performance at Glastonbury, Stormzy wore a custom-made stab-proof vest by Banksy to highlight the knife-crime crisis that overwhelmingly affects Black men in Britain.

'FASHION FUNCTIONS AS A MIRROR TO OUR TIMES, SO IT IS INHERENTLY POLITICAL. IT'S BEEN USED TO EXPRESS PATRIOTIC, NATIONALISTIC, AND PROPAGANDISTIC TENDENCIES AS WELL AS COMPLEX ISSUES RELATED TO CLASS, RACE, ETHNICITY, GENDER, AND SEXUALITY.'

ANDREW BOLTON

SOCIAL MEDIA MATTERS

With the ubiquity of smart phones and the introduction of new social media apps, from Twitter to Instagram, Snapchat and TikTok, images were disseminated faster than ever before. The 2010s saw a rise in social media influencers who could connect with their fans directly and set instant fashions through the images they shared on their own channels. The Kardashians, who found fame through reality television, launched billion-dollar fashion businesses and crossed over onto the prestigious pages of *Vogue*, a space normally out of bounds for reality stars. Kim Kardashian also made headlines with her appearances at the prestigious Met Gala, such as in a skin-tight, wet-look Thierry Mugler gown.

While social media had, at first, been hailed as a way for people around the world to connect, a dark side soon emerged with vicious comments and hateful campaigns targeted at the famous and non-famous alike. In 2015 reality stars Blac Chyna and Amber Rose appeared at the MTV Video Music Awards dressed in custom-made bodysuits printed with the slut-shaming words they had been called on social media.

WEARING YOUR HEART ON YOUR SLEEVE – OR HEAD

By 2016 it seemed that people had formed their own political tribes marked out by visual signifiers, including the red MAGA hat, worn by supporters of President Donald Trump and the pink 'pussy' hats collectively worn at the women's marches in 2017. Slogan T-shirts were an increasingly popular way of delivering political messages of support, from Dior's high-end 'We Should All Be Feminists' and Otherwild's 'The Future Is Female', to Black Lives Matter slogans such as 'I Can't Breathe', as worn by sport stars like the late Kobe Bryant.

Concerns around global warming, coupled with extreme weather conditions, has led to criticism of the fashion industry in terms of its environmental impact. While fast fashion fitted with the instant gratification of social media, there is an increased interest in developing sustainable fabrics that are not as exploitative on the environment. The way people wish to consume fashion is ever changing, and new innovations such as spider silk and mushroom leather are opening up new opportunities for the industry. And with the power of social media, and the lightning-quick way images are disseminated and go viral, fashion is changing faster than ever before.

2009
→   President Barack Obama is sworn into office and First Lady Michelle Obama becomes a socially-conscious style icon. She champions independent American designers like Narciso Rodriguez and Jason Wu.

2010
→   Instagram is launched as a photo-sharing social network and gains one million registered users in two months.
→   Lady Gaga appears at the MTV Music Video Awards in a dress constructed from raw meat.

2011
→   Model Andreja Pejić causes controversy as the first androgynous model on a magazine cover for *Dossier Journal*.
→   A year after the death of Alexander McQueen, the Metropolitan Museum of Art holds a retrospective exhibition of his work, Savage Beauty.
→   Street-style photographer Phil Oh shoots his first fashion week for *Vogue*.
→   Cara Delevingne makes her catwalk debut for Burberry at London Fashion Week, becoming the It model of the next decade.

2012
→   Facebook buys Instagram for 1 billion dollars.

2013
→   Pyer Moss is founded by New York-based designer Kerby Jean-Raymond.
→   The collapse of the Rana Plaza garment factory in Bangladesh forces the fashion industry to take a hard look at the exploitation of its workers.

2016
→   Bill Cunningham, the father of street-style photography, passes away.
→   Britain votes to leave the European Union.
→   Ashley Graham is the first plus-size model to appear on the cover of *Sports Illustrated*, heralding a new body inclusivity.
→   The Black Lives Matter movement goes global to protest police violence.

2017
→   Kim Kardashian founds her beauty line KKW Beauty in 2017, helping to shape a new aesthetic and demonstrating the power of influencers.
→   Women's marches are held across the United States as a response to the inauguration of President Donald Trump.

→ Maria Grazia Chiuri launches the 'We Should All Be Feminists' T-shirt for Christian Dior.
→ Stella McCartney announces a new partnership with biotechnology company Bolt Threads to create the next generation of ethical fabrics.
→ Edward Enninful is appointed as the first Black male editor-in-chief of British *Vogue*.
→ Rihanna shakes up the beauty industry with the launch of her Fenty Beauty line, with a foundation range of forty shades.

2018
→ Janelle Monáe releases the music video for 'Pynk', featuring pairs of 'vagina' pants.

2019
→ *Pose* star Billy Porter defies convention by wearing a gown, rather than a tuxedo, to the Academy Awards.

2020
→ The Covid-19 pandemic triggers a global lockdown and fashion weeks around the world are cancelled.
→ Further Black Lives Matter protests and riots erupt across the world as a result of the killing of African-American George Floyd at the hands of a Minneapolis police officer on 25 May. As the focus on racial inequality comes under scrutiny, the fashion industry reflects on its diversity and inclusivity.
→ TikTok for Business is launched, helping to push fashion on the app.
→ Following the ripple effect of the murder of George Floyd and the Black Lives Matter protests, British *Vogue* features supermodel Adwoa Aboah on the front cover of the September issue, dressed all in black.

2021
→ Bold block-colour coats make their appearance at the presidential inauguration of Joe Biden in January.
→ Plus-size model Precious Lee is signed by Versace to model the Medusa handbag.

2022
→ Spring Fashion Month was named the most diverse, with 48 per cent of appearances by models of colour, and transgender, non-binary and plus-size representations.

THE RED MEAT OF MUSIC

LADY GAGA'S MEAT DRESS
FRANC FERNANDEZ
2010

When Lady Gaga came on stage to accept her award for Video of the Year for 'Bad Romance' at the 2010 Video Music Awards, she created the most outrageous fashion moment of the night, and possibly of the year. The dress was entirely constructed from real red meat, which the Argentine designer of the dress, Franc Fernandez, proudly announced was 'from my family butcher', using a cut of meat known as *matambre*, which preserves well.

In her meteoric rise as avant-garde pop princess, Lady Gaga had made a name for herself with her surrealist, conversation-provoking costumes, such as meeting Queen Elizabeth II in red PVC, encasing herself in an egg sculpture at the 2011 Grammy Awards and a dramatic white Francesco Scognamiglio cape with a Philip Treacy headpiece for the 2010 Brit Awards. She had previously worn a meat bikini for the front cover of *Vogue* Japan in 2010, but she and her stylist Nicola Formichetti chose to take the concept even further.

It was her third costume change of the night for the 2010 VMAs, and the next day the meat dress was the dominant image as it was splashed across newspapers around the world, with one question being asked again and again – what does it mean? Some suggestions included that it was a feminist statement around women being a commodity, like meat, or that it represented ageing and decay. The meat dress was particularly controversial in its provocation of the growing vegan movement, with People for the Ethical Treatment of Animals (PETA) condemning the dress, as did the Vegetarian Society.

Gaga later revealed on the Ellen DeGeneres show that 'it has many interpretations, but for me this evening … If we don't stand up for what we believe in and if we don't fight for our rights, pretty soon we're going to have as much rights as the meat on our own bones. And I am not a piece of meat.' In particular, she said the dress was a statement to protest the US military's Don't Ask, Don't Tell policy, which discriminated against gay men and women serving in the army. She later said it referenced a speech she gave, which she called 'The Prime Rib of America', in which she defended LGBTQ + rights.

The dress would remain part of fashion history, with questions as to what happened to it, and if it was ever eaten. Fernandez claimed that it went through a preservation process to create a 'jerky', so that it would be kept in Gaga's fashion archive.

Lady Gaga in Franc Fernandez's meat dress at the 2010 MTV Video Music Awards.

PROTEST, RESISTANCE AND SOCIAL MEDIA 2008–PRESENT

ANDROGYNOUS CONTROVERSY

ANDREJA PEJIĆ'S COVER
DOSSIER JOURNAL
2011

After being scouted at a Melbourne swimming pool in her final year of high school, Bosnian-Herzegovinian-born Andreja Pejić rose to fame as the world's first androgynous model. Having crossed over into both men's and women's shows for designers like Marc Jacobs and Jean Paul Gaultier, it seemed a natural next step for Pejić to appear on the cover of *Dossier Journal* in 2011, in androgynous guise: topless, with hair in curlers. In an interview with Australia's *Sunday Night*, on the Seven Network, Pejić laughed: 'I think in times of recession and economic collapse I don't think clients have much money to hire both men and women, so I'm really a good deal.'

When the issue hit the newsstands it caused immediate confusion and controversy because of the ambiguity as to whether a topless woman was appearing on the cover. *Dossier Journal* received further publicity with reports that Barnes & Noble bookshop had asked for all copies of the cover to be placed in opaque polybags, usually reserved for porn, because the gender-provoking image was too controversial for American audiences. The feminist website Jezebel reacted in annoyance at the double standards. 'He's not a fitness model, a well-muscled leading man actor, or a buff musician. Does the Barnes & Noble newsstand have a minimum biceps standard, no skinny dudes need apply?'

Two years after she was splashed on the cover of *Dossier Journal*, Pejić underwent sex reassignment surgery and came out as a trans woman, changing her name from Andrej to Andreja. But at the time of the cover, Pejić identified as male. Pejić told *New York* magazine in 2011: 'I think the question really isn't the gender of the person on the cover, it's whether it's porn or it's art. And clearly, it's art, so art really should not be censored in a democratic society.'

Pejić continued to make headlines and break barriers. In May 2015 she became the first openly transgender model profiled by *Vogue*, with the headline: 'Has the Fashion Industry Reached a Transgender Turning Point?' As the first transgender model to be the face of a make-up brand, after signing with Make Up Forever, and as the first transgender woman to appear on the cover of *GQ*, the *Dossier Journal* cover marked a turning point for gender fluidity and the mainstreaming of transgender identity.

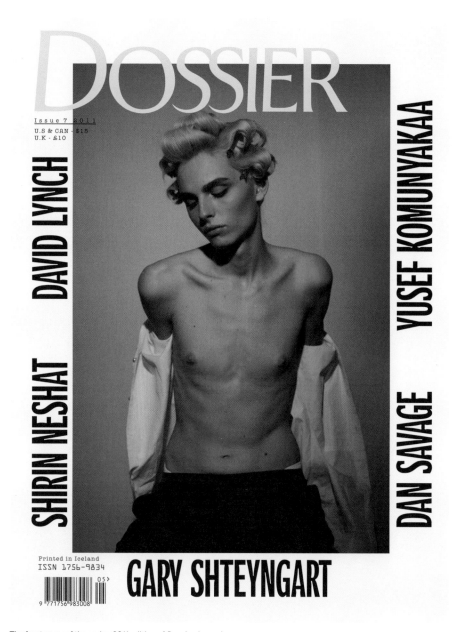

DOSSIER

Issue 7 2011
U.S & CAN - $15
U.K - £10

DAVID LYNCH

YUSEF KOMUNYAKAA

SHIRIN NESHAT

DAN SAVAGE

Printed in Iceland
ISSN 1756-9834

GARY SHTEYNGART

The front cover of the spring 2011 edition of *Dossier Journal*.

STEPPING AWAY FROM
THE FASHION REALM

STEPDANCERS
RICK OWENS
2014

When Rick Owens chose to showcase his spring–summer 2014 collection on the bodies of Black women as they performed a stepdance, he was praised for challenging the norms of the fashion industry by rejecting the standard model aesthetic in favour of under-represented women.

The California-born designer, known for his 'health-goth' style, hired four sorority stepdance groups from across the United States to take on the dual role of performing in and modelling his black leather gillets, headpieces and jackets for his collection entitled Vicious.

Stepdancing evolved from fraternity and sorority groups at African-American colleges, mixing tap, cheerleading and military drill into an assertive dance, which sometimes involves contorting the face into grimaces. The show was immediately praised for capturing a moment of reckoning for the fashion industry, following the 2013 publication of an open letter from Naomi Campbell, Iman and Bethann Hardison to major fashion houses raising concerns over the lack of Black and Asian models on British catwalks.

Fashion blogger Susie Bubble hailed Owens for making 'the most powerful and provocative statement this season'; *Dazed* asked if it was 'the beginning of a revolution' and *Vogue* said of the show: 'all those body types today added up to as inclusive a catwalk vision of womanhood as we're ever likely to see. Such a gentle notion, and yet it struck home with a sledgehammer force.'

Despite the applause for his inclusivity, Owens was also criticized for his use of the word 'vicious' in a show that used predominantly Black women to model his clothes. In an interview with *Racked* magazine, San Francisco dancer Amara Tabor-Smith found it problematic in its depiction of Black women, because 'it was obvious that it was intended to shake up or to maybe shock the audience – those who attend fashion shows'.

One of the dancers of the show, New York-based Arin Lawrence, spoke to Buzzfeed about her performance, and of the pressure to put on a 'grit face'. 'It was a struggle, certainly. We were all told, you have to make these faces.' But she said, 'We all felt that this was a huge opportunity for it to be presented on the world stage in an unconventional way, and just to widen the scope of anyone who sees and hears about it. If I go on Instagram and search for "Rick Owens" now there's a lot about us there, which is weird – but good weird.'

Stepdancers at Rick Owens spring–summer 2014 fashion show in Paris.

INSTANT GRATIFICATION

FAST FOOD COLLECTION
JEREMY SCOTT FOR MOSCHINO
2014

For his debut autumn–winter 2014 ready-to-wear collection for Moschino, Jeremy Scott embraced consumer culture with his bright and brash designs that gave a humorous twist to recognizable junk food brands with word play and reconfigured logos. He adapted Moschino's heart design into McDonald's golden arches, printing it onto Happy Meal handbags, which were served up on a tray by model Anna Ewers in a uniform-esque beige-and-red shirtwaist dress and sun visor, and created baggy red sweaters with an 'M' for Moschino over the slogan 'Over 20 Billion Served'.

Moschino is a brand that has a long tradition of mixing high fashion with bad taste, poking fun at the fashion industry through its tongue-in-cheek designs. When Franco Moschino launched the label in 1983, he sought to disrupt elite fashions by taking their symbols and infusing them with pop art and transforming Chanel's elegant hats into blow-up beach toys.

For his junk food collection, Scott paid tribute to the late Franco (who was sued by Chanel back in the 1980s for his mockery of the brand) by borrowing the classic Chanel silhouette of slim-fit jackets and skirts, but making them pop in bold yellow and red. As well as adapting the instantly recognisable McDonald's branding, Scott featured popcorn mini-dresses, SpongeBob SquarePants jersey dresses, sweaters and accessories, and ballgowns appearing as if constructed from chocolate bars and crisp packets.

When he was appointed head of the Italian fashion house in 2013, Scott had already demonstrated his obsession with food in fashion. For his eponymous label's autumn–winter 2006 Food Fight collection, models were dressed as slices of pizza, wrapped like a chocolate bar and wearing a corset that resembled a Mr Whippy cone. Scott told British *Vogue*: 'Breakfast cereals and chocolate bars are all part of our collective conscience, so they are immediately recognisable, familiar and understood. I love to work with iconography for that very reason. It's a shared visual language which allows me to communicate to more people.'

The day after the collection launch, a ten-piece capsule collection entitled Next Day After the Runway went on sale, and the sweaters and Happy Meal handbags, having been snapped up by Katy Perry, Jourdan Dunn and other influencers, quickly sold out. Such was the impact of Scott's debut collection, five months later debate was still raging as to whether his show encouraged unhealthy eating. While there was irony in an industry criticised for super-slim models now being taken to task for encouraging obesity, health campaigners came out in protest against glorifying junk food.

Jeremy Scott's riff on the McDonald's logo at Moschino's autumn–winter 2014 Milan show.

PROTEST, RESISTANCE AND SOCIAL MEDIA 2008–PRESENT

One of the items that came in for particular criticism was the Moschino iPhone case in the shape of McDonald's french fries. Months after the show, the cases were popular with fashion editors, bloggers and celebrities like Rihanna and Rita Ora, and counterfeit versions were quickly rushed out. Obesity expert and GP Dr Ian Campbell was quoted in *The Observer* as expressing concerns for children using these iPhone cases and 'buying in to the whole fast-food concept', 'while the occasional McDonald's meal is not a problem, to present it as fashion is disappointing.'

Grazia magazine wrote in defence: 'Moschino isn't sexualising fast food here. We aren't talking about McDonald's-esque crotchless panties ... The entire collection is infinitely more fun and kitsch than it is sexually alluring – unlike the adverts of many fast food chains.'

There was a barrage of further criticism when a March 2014 article in the *Daily Mail* also claimed that fast food workers were insulted by Scott's witty, high-end designs while they struggled on minimum wage. Despite the censure, Scott would later say of his debut collection: 'I hold the McDonald's collection very near and dear to my heart, because of my love of symbols.'

Scott's collection also sparked a trend for mouth watering food to inspire fashion and for people to wear their favourite junk food on their body. Scott further played with the camp food iconography for the 2019 Met Ball, when he dressed Katy Perry in a succulent 3-D burger dress, and for the Brit Awards 2020 when he dressed popstar Lizzo as a bar of chocolate, an outfit adapted from his 2014 collection.

'THERE'S THIS TERM IN THE INDUSTRY, OF COURSE, "FAST FASHION" – BUT I WANTED TO DO A NEW CONCEPT THAT MADE IT FASTER, LIKE MCDONALD'S.'

JEREMY SCOTT

In the 2010s the fashion industry shifted towards greater diversity in their representation of different body shapes, following scrutiny around their narrow depictions of beauty. These changes were pushed by campaign groups and social media movements, such as fourth-wave feminism, and a renewed sense of activism among Generation Z.

As advertising began to reflect a need for body positivity, a new generation of models challenged the status quo. In 2016, Ashley Graham became the first plus-size model to appear on a *Sports Illustrated* cover. Paloma Elsesser walked the catwalks in 2021 for Fendi and Ferragamo, and was hired by Coach for their Originals Go Their Own Way campaign. After being discovered by make-up artist Pat McGrath in 2015, she found that some brands needed persuading to change their representation. 'Sometimes they don't see that [larger] can be elevated and chic,' Elsesser told *Vogue* in December 2020, as the magazine's cover star. 'If they aren't seeing images of girls in magazines, they aren't going to think about them for the campaigns.'

Precious Lee was signed for the Versace spring-summer 2021 campaign to model the Medusa handbag. While some brands are still limited in their sizing, despite the representation, Versace announced their dedication to making available every look by 'plus-size' models up to a UK size 20. 'One thing goes with the other,' said Donatella Versace. 'What is the point of having different body sizes on the catwalk if then those same girls won't find those clothes when they go shopping at Versace?'

A MIRROR TO THE WORLD

From Zandra Rhodes' Punk collection to Anna Sui's tributes to grunge, fashion designers have frequently looked to street style to find inspiration for their collections, and some, like Vivienne Westwood and Katharine Hamnett, have been at the forefront of resistance fashion, picking up on a sense of change in the air to politicize their collections.

Clothing is an instant visualiser, often the first thing people notice, and so stylistic imagery is a powerful method of making a statement of resistance. The suffragettes followed contemporary aesthetics to look feminine while fighting for women's rights, and during the Vietnam War, protesters played with the rules of the armed forces to fight against it, such as growing their hair long or wearing army jackets with messages scrawled on them.

There hasn't been as prescient a time as the 2010s and 2020s, when politics and fashion have become so intertwined. This connection has been triggered by a continuing wave of concerns and crises that have come to the fore and which have been highlighted globally due to the power of social media. These include Black Lives Matter, particularly following the murder of George Floyd, the #MeToo movement and its almost daily allegations of sexual misconduct, pressures from the Brexit vote in Britain, the election and presidency of Donald Trump in 2016 and the outbreak of a global pandemic in 2020.

Over the past couple of years, fashion labels have co-opted the resistance message, such as by using the black berets of the Black Panthers, or slogans such as 'I Can't Breathe' and 'We Should All Be Feminists' printed onto T-shirts and onto the skin of their models, echoing those who use them to campaign on the streets. But does the message become watered down when commoditized, and adopted by the mainstream? Social consciousness and environmental concerns are now having a major impact on the direction of designers and fashion brands, whether that's from genuine concern about issues that matter or as part of an advertising campaign to capture the mood in the air.

(Left) Pyer Moss's spring 2019 collection, (Right) Burberry's Pride collection.

The logo T-shirt may have been the simplest way to put forward a political message, much like the sandwich boards worn in the 1930s, but since 2016 designers have stepped up in bringing strong statements to the runway by creating immersive experiences to their shows. Pyer Moss was an early instigator in using his fashion to protest the Black Lives Matter movement, from his 2015 'They Have Names' T-shirt to his revolutionary 2016 show, and his documentation of Black history in his 2019 show. Burberry, in 2018, created a Pride collection, which used the rainbow stripes of the LGBTQ+ to reinvent their famous check, while supporting three charities dedicated to those communities around the world.

'Fashion functions as a mirror to our times, so it is inherently political,' Andrew Bolton, curator in charge of the Costume Institute at the Metropolitan Museum of Art, told *Vogue*. 'It's been used to express patriotic, nationalistic, and propagandistic tendencies as well as complex issues related to class, race, ethnicity, gender, and sexuality.'

BRINGING BLACK LIVES MATTER TO THE RUNWAY

BLACK LIVES MATTER VIDEO AND SHOW
PYER MOSS
2015

In 2015, Kerby Jean-Raymond, founder of design label Pyer Moss, took the Black Lives Matter movement to the runway. The powerful messaging caused such controversy that it led to death threats against the designer and real concern that he might go out of business. America wasn't ready for being confronted so directly by a Black designer about the African-American experience.

At the time, it seemed there were constant headlines about deaths of Black men in custody, and with concern around unanswered police brutality, protests were breaking out across America, with slogans such as 'I Can't Breathe', and the names of those who died – Eric Garner, Marlon Brown – etched on skin. Jean-Raymond had launched Pyer Moss in 2013, but his decision to use his platform to speak out on such a contentious issue, almost led to his label being shut down. He said, 'I knew I wouldn't be able to sleep at night if I didn't address these issues. I was prepared for it to be my last show.'

Jean-Raymond's spring–summer 2016 show opened at New York Fashion Week with a powerful twelve-minute video featuring interviews with the family members of those who had been killed and with real clips of police brutality. It was designed to give a sharp shock to the fashion editors in the audience, who weren't normally thinking of these deep concerns, and thrust it into their consciousness.

Screening such a politically charged video was a big risk, and he and his team struggled to find a suitable venue, with a number of places declining on the back of the show's messaging. Instead they had to go with the Altman Building on 18th Street, paying way over their budget. With the sky-high costs, and the concern that it could be the end of the brand, Raymond and his team considered cancelling.

It was an interaction with the police right before his show, however, that convinced the designer to go ahead. As he later recounted, 'Right outside my apartment in Southside Jamaica, Queens, I had a cast on my hand, was talking to my sister on the phone, was coming in from buying a beef patty, and I look up and I hear, "Put it down, put it down!" And these cops had their guns drawn on me.'

The video brought the room to complete silence, and once it was finished, the audience appeared in shock, some gasping, some crying. Following the impact of the video, diverse models came out dressed in a military style that featured

A slogan jacket at Pyer Moss's spring 2016 New York Fashion Week show.

PROTEST, RESISTANCE AND SOCIAL MEDIA 2008–PRESENT

messages of the movement, such as a khaki coat with 'I Can't Breathe' on the back and work boots painted with the names of those killed by the police.

The show was one of the first times a designer had been so confrontational in delivering a message to his audience. It was well received by the fashion press, with fashion writer Robin Givhan from *The Washington Post* helping to thrust the little-known label into the spotlight.

However the press attention soon provoked the simmering rage of white supremacists, who sent threats to the designer over social media and placed him on a 'target' list. It also led to some stores dropping his label.

'Within thirty-six hours, six of my biggest accounts dropped me,' he told Vogue Business. He was also thrown into legal wrangles with investors, leading to anxiety and panic attacks. 'People were recognising me now on the train – I was broke and famous, and it was really scary.'

When Jean-Raymond received a call from musician Erykah Badu, encouraging him to persevere, he was emboldened to work on a new show for spring–summer 2017, this time dealing with mental health. From there he spring-boarded to success, with a deal under Reebok and with Vice-President Kamala Harris choosing one of his designs, a camel coat with a wave design, for inauguration week.

His shows, continuing the theme of the African-American experience, also received critical acclaim, and in 2021 he became the first Black American designer to show at Paris Fashion Week, with his surrealist couture. Following the death in custody of George Floyd, businesses were desperate to appear supportive of the Black Lives Matter movement, but it was Pyer Moss that delivered an important message in having courage of conviction before that.

'I KNEW I WOULDN'T BE ABLE TO SLEEP AT NIGHT IF I DIDN'T ADDRESS THESE ISSUES. I WAS PREPARED FOR IT TO BE MY LAST SHOW.'

KERBY JEAN-RAYMOND

Pink pussy hats on display at the Women's March in Washington, 2017.

An image can speak a thousand words, and this concept was used to powerful effect in the new age of protest in the 2010s onwards. Activists took to the streets to campaign for equality and civil rights abuses in such movements as #MeToo, against sexual misconduct against women, and Black Lives Matter, highlighting among other things the deaths in custody of Black men and women.

Clothing is one of the ways individuals and groups can challenge and rebel against the dominant position, whether that's related to gender, class or race. During protests, simple items, such as the pink pussy hats at women's marches or the yellow vests when worn by thousands of demonstrators in France to protest against rising prices of fuel, became an instantly recognisable visual. With their accessibility, they were an easy way to show solidarity.

At Black Lives Matter rallies, protestors dressed completely in black, standing in silence, their hands in the air, some with tape over their mouths, some with slogans or the names of those killed by police – Eric Garner, Walter Scott, George Floyd, among others – written on T-shirts. Words and clothing collided together in this movement, as with others, with strong messages playing an important part in the visuals. These messages became an effective tool in raising awareness, as their power lies in the way a simple slogan can be carried and worn by a mass of people and quickly disseminated across social media.

THE NEW FASHION FOR FEMINISM

WE SHOULD ALL BE FEMINISTS T-SHIRT
MARIA GRAZIA CHIURI FOR DIOR
2016

In September 2016, Maria Grazia Chiuri marked her debut show as the first-ever female creative director of Christian Dior by making a strong feminist statement with cotton T-shirts branded with the words 'We Should All Be Feminists'. The slogan was borrowed directly from leading Nigerian author Chimamanda Ngozi Adichie's 2014 groundbreaking essay of the same name. An adaptation of Adichie's 2012 inspirational TED talk, it gained further traction when Beyoncé featured an extract in her 2013 song 'Flawless'.

Models walked the runway at Paris Fashion Week for Dior's spring–summer 2017 ready-to-wear collection wearing the crisp cotton T-shirts with sheer tulle ballet skirts. While they harked back to the popularity of the 'J'adore Dior' T-shirts under John Galliano's leadership, the feminist messaging became a favourite statement item on Instagram feeds, for street style, and worn by outspoken feminist celebrities Natalie Portman, Jennifer Lawrence and Rihanna.

The launch of Dior's feminist statement T-shirt coincided with an upsurge in concern around women's issues. It was fuelled by the election to the US presidency of Donald Trump in January 2017, and the global #MeToo campaign in October 2017, sparked by serious allegations of repeated sexual misconduct against Hollywood producer Harvey Weinstein.

From 'This Is What a Feminist Looks Like' to 'Nevertheless, She Persisted', T-shirts with feminist slogans had become a popular statement from 2015. In October of that year, Cara Delevingne was pictured in a navy sweatshirt with the slogan 'The Future Is Female', and later that month, her girlfriend at the time, Annie Clark, known as the musician St Vincent, was pictured in the same shirt at the Chateau Marmont in Hollywood. The sweatshirt became a hot talking point on Instagram and Tumblr, and while it seemed a very modern statement, it was first conceived by second-wave feminists in the 1970s. The original was created by New York City's first women's bookstore, Labyris Books, and was captured by photographer Liza Cowan in an image of her girlfriend Alix Dobkin wearing the T-shirt in 1975. The image popped up in 2015 on the Instagram account Herstory, and it led to the slogan being printed on a shirt by Rachel Berks, owner of a Los Angeles graphic design studio.

For Rome-born Chiuri, she chose to make a strong statement as the first woman to lead the direction of Dior. 'Dior is feminine,' she told *The Guardian*. 'That's what I kept hearing when I told people I was coming here. But as a woman, "feminine" means something different to me than it means to a man, perhaps. Feminine is about being a woman, no? I thought to myself: If Dior is

The We Should all be Feminists t-shirt as street style, at Paris Fashion Week 2017.

about femininity, then it is about women. And not about what it was to be a woman fifty years ago, but to be a woman today.'

The Dior slogan T-shirt was high fashion, yet was designed to work at street level. Retailing at £560, its expense was divisive, leading to criticism that it was out of the reach of most people. Further, the label was accused of co-opting the street-level feminist protests. In response, Dior announced in February 2017 that an undisclosed percentage of proceeds from the profits would go to the Clara Lionel Foundation, Rihanna's non-profit organization.

Despite the criticism of the T-shirts, Chiuri received the blessing of Adichie, a guest of honour at the September 2016 show, for the use of the slogan on Dior's T-shirts. 'A T-shirt is not going to change the world, right? But, I think change happens when we spread ideas,' said Adichie. We have a young generation who are also thinking about sexism. We have young women who have experienced things, but they don't have the language. If you have a T-shirt that says "feminist", it's giving them an entry to having a language to talk about things they have already experienced.'

'A T-SHIRT IS NOT GOING TO CHANGE THE WORLD, RIGHT? BUT, I THINK CHANGE HAPPENS WHEN WE SPREAD IDEAS.'

CHIMAMANDA NGOZI ADICHIE

One of the biggest shake-ups in fashion in the twenty-first century was the influence of Instagram: it shifted the power from fashion brands to real people, 'influencers' who could wield power by accruing millions of followers. The app shaped a new visual for 2010 of bright, kitsch colours that created an idealised version of reality, which was both aspirational and envy-inducing.

By 2019 it had grown to one million users and had earned a reputation for staged lifestyle photos with brightly coloured backdrops, bodies swathed in revealing clothing, the contour make-up look made famous by the Kardashians and close-ups of perfectly arranged portions of avocado toast. It was here that influencers shaped a new look for fashion, where the aesthetic of matte lips, lash extensions and sculpted eyebrows became predominant.

Marketing was shaped around what would look good on Instagram, with museums and events aware of how they could take advantage of need to share to followers. There was the pop-up Museum of Ice Cream in New York and an LA Instagram museum called Happy Place, which launched in 2017 by billing itself as the 'most Instagrammable pop-up in America'.

As people became more savvy to the marketing on Instagram, the fake set-ups, filters and the non-declared promotions, users on the app shifted towards a trend for Instagram vs reality photos, allowing influencers to show themselves in a more revealing, and less artificial, light. Fashion houses continue to be aware of the power of Instagram, and while influencers must now declare sponsored posts, it's still a powerful tool in shaping future aesthetics as consumers can effectively curate their own fashion moodboards to find inspiration for their outfits.

THE RISE OF STREET STYLE

Over the last ten years there has been a growing trend for capturing fashion on the street, led by the late *New York Times* photographer Bill Cunningham and his On the Street column, and Scott Schuman's The Sartorialist, which also captured New York's stylish denizens before branching out to other cities around the world. Street style has proved to be a source of inspiration for creating attainable style when couture is out of reach for most people.

While early street-style pioneers like Ted Polhemus captured raw subcultural images in the 1970s and 1980s, showcasing the unique DIY style of punks, rockabillies and mod-revivalists, the new concept of street style was much more polished and high level. Rather than expressing a sense of teenage angst, it showcased everyday fashion as high concept.

Through the development of digital media, street style grew from depicting ordinary people dressing in interesting ways, to a more eye-catching, bolder aesthetic where it became a lucrative business in itself. *Vogue*'s Phil Oh first began shooting street style at fashion weeks in 2011, and this further evolved when a new type of fashion journalist, bloggers like Susie Lau and Leandra Medine of Man Repeller, began appearing in street style coverage, as they secured coveted positions on the front row, or 'frow', of fashion shows. It was a democratization of fashion, opening up access from Hollywood stars and socialites to ordinary people who had a flair for fashion and social media.

It became a ritual at the twice-yearly fashion weeks around the world, from Paris to New York, London to Tokyo, to see a display of powerful influencers and It girls such as Chiara Ferragni and Olivia Palermo, peacocking outside the hottest shows in clothing that was often gifted to them, and where their images would be disseminated to their hundreds of thousands of followers on Instagram.

In 2013 fashion journalist Suzy Menkes in *The New York Times* lambasted street style for becoming a spectacle. 'Cameras point as wildly at their prey as those original paparazzi in Fellini's *La Dolce Vita*. But

Fashion bloggers (left) Susie Lau, aka Susie Bubble (right) Leandra Medine of Man Repeller.

now subjects are ready and willing to be objects, not so much hunted down by the paparazzi as gagging for their attention,' she wrote. 'There is a genuine difference between the stylish and the showoffs – and that is the current dilemma. If fashion is for everyone, is it fashion?'

The phenomenon gained further notoriety with a scathing round-table article that appeared in *Vogue* in 2016, in which the editors criticised the street style at Milan Fashion Week. They targeted the influencers as 'pathetic' and 'sad'. It led to a conversation around the conflict between organic style from the street and the fashion that magazines like *Vogue* sell.

There may be different opinions on what street style should be, but what's clear is that the style of the guests at fashion week is just as important as what's being shown on the catwalk.

DETAILS OF DYSTOPIA

THE BALACLAVA
RAF SIMONS FOR CALVIN KLEIN
2018

Raf Simons is a designer known as a provocateur. For his autumn–winter 2018 collection for Calvin Klein, shown at New York Fashion Week, he used knitted balaclavas as a deliberate commentary on the political unrest in the United States and overseas. His use of the balaclava coincided with an upturn in interest in the headgear, as seen in Beyoncé and Jay-Z's 2014 On the Run tour, and Cara Delevingne wearing a balaclava with the lettering BS in September 2013, which she declared as 'fashion anarchy'.

Belgian-born Raf Simons paired his balaclavas with orange hazmat suits, *Little House on the Prairie* gingham gowns and 50,000 gallons of popcorn covering the floor of the American Stock Exchange, where the show was held, for an apocalyptic apparition.

While it was initially designed to keep the head protected from the cold, the balaclava has taken on a dystopian aesthetic, when used in anti-government protests to help disguise appearances and to make a visual statement. The balaclava originated during the Crimean War when women in Britain knitted head coverings for the men being sent to Balaclava, Ukraine, but by the 1970s anarchists in Germany were wearing them to fight the police. Russian feminist punks Pussy Riot delivered an anti-Putin message dressed in neon balaclavas, hiding their identity like political bandits. Because of the anonymity that it offers, and the way it's also been used by criminals, the balaclava has become associated with the subversive.

As well as continuing with his own Antwerp-based menswear line, Simons took over as chief creative officer of Calvin Klein in August 2016, with the aim of shaking up the brand. But by the end of 2018, he was ousted by Calvin Klein. His vision contrasted with the ethos of the billion-dollar business, which was simple, sexy and casual, and despite the publicity around his high-concept shows, Simons' designs didn't translate into sales.

Despite this, his apocalyptic balaclavas and hazmats caught the mood of the times and were picked up by other designers like Gucci, Alexander Wang, Celine and Vetements. They seemed particularly prophetic following the worldwide Covid-19 pandemic, when they were hailed by *Harper's Bazaar* in February 2021 as the comfortable and warm way to wear face masks. According to *The Guardian*, online searches for the term rose 59 per cent between 2019 and 2020, and as *The Wall Street Journal* that same month noted: 'In the era of widespread face coverings, the curious and sometimes menacing balaclava has surged in popularity.'

Raf Simon's balaclava at Calvin Klein's autumn–winter 2018 collection.

PROTEST, RESISTANCE AND SOCIAL MEDIA 2008–PRESENT

RECLAIMING PINK POWER

JANELLE MONÁE'S VAGINA PANTS
DURAN LANTINK
2018

As millennial women embraced a new wave of feminism, they wanted to take ownership of their body parts, especially at a time of reckoning with the #MeToo movement. Gwyneth Paltrow launched a candle emblazoned with the words 'This smells like my vagina', women wore pussy hats at the 2017 women's marches to protest President Trump's abuse of the word in the infamous *Access Hollywood* tapes, and Cara Delevingne gave *Architectural Digest* a tour of her LA home, complete with a vagina tunnel with padded pink walls. But the fashion design that fully captured the moment was the vagina pants in Janelle Monáe's 2018 music video for 'Pynk'. Created by Amsterdam designer Duran Lantink, they encased the legs with pale-pink-and-fuchsia frills to form labia.

Gynaecological art is not a new phenomenon – Georgia O'Keeffe denied that the pink flowers in her paintings were designed to look like vulvas – but the vagina pants are the most wearable of these creations, and serve as a way of taking power back after the fetishisation of female bodies for so long.

Lantink was drafted in to work on the music video by the director, Emma Westernberg, five days before the shoot. 'I have no idea what vaginas are, I mean, I'm gay,' he told the BBC. 'So I started right away Googling vaginas ... I went to this Indian silk shop where this lady was standing ... "We said we have this particular pink that is inside a vagina or around a vagina?"'

The pants perfectly symbolised the message of the song, to celebrate female power, 'no matter if you have a vagina or not', as Monáe stated on Twitter. In the video, filmed in the pink-tinted desert, Monáe and her backing dancers drive pink convertibles, showcase knickers with the words 'I Grab Back' and stand in formation with their arms linked and their legs moving apart, to create a vision of pink vulvas opening and closing.

As the video went viral, the vagina pants became the most talked about piece of clothing of the year. Items in the press featured interviews with Monáe who spoke of her desire to mass-manufacture them. As well as celebrating the vagina, they also demonstrated how pink wasn't just sweet and feminine, but could be strong and powerful, a colour fit for a new generation of women who were confrontational and unafraid to talk about their bodies and their sexuality.

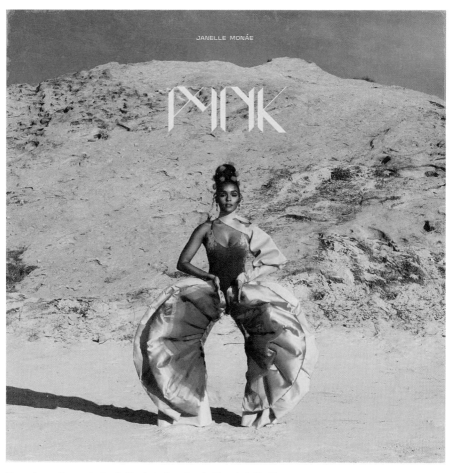

The vagina pants worn by Janelle Monáe for the artwork of her single 'Pynk'.

PROTEST, RESISTANCE AND SOCIAL MEDIA 2008–PRESENT

FUTURISTIC FABRICS

MYLO FABRIC
STELLA MCCARTNEY AND BOLT THREADS
2021

In March 2021, Stella McCartney unveiled the first garment made from an innovative new fabric from San Francisco biotechnology company Bolt Threads – a mushroom-based, vegan leather named Mylo. It was hailed as the future of sustainable fabrics.

Since she launched her fashion label in 2001, Stella McCartney has promoted her own environmental awareness and drive for sustainable fashion, with a commitment to refrain from using leather, feathers or fur in her designs. As a lifelong vegan, and inspired by her mother, Linda, who launched her own range of vegetarian food and cookbooks, McCartney has long been outspoken about the damage to the planet of processing leather, which is linked to global warming, deforestation and water pollution. Fur-free fur has been part of her collections for years, and she uses recycled wool and cashmere, along with a polyester made from recycled plastic bottles. She has also looked to a new generation of fabrics designed to be recyclable, ecological and renewable, such as Mylo.

Bolt Threads was founded in 2009 by bioengineers in the San Francisco Bay area of California, creating a new, ecological way of developing silk. Using yeast to encourage microorganisms to excrete silk proteins, it created ultra-strong silk that could be woven or knitted into cloth. In 2017 McCartney teamed up with Bolt Threads to make a golden dress from this Microsilk, for a display at the Museum of Modern Art in New York. It was the first new fabric in decades, and was designed to be the future of ethical fashion, as the fabric is able to break down naturally when discarded. While the spider silk wasn't at a stage where it could compete with fabrics like polyester for its price and durability, Bolt Threads championed their mushroom leather as the future of sustainable fashion.

The concept isn't new. The spongy fabric Amadou, created from a fungal tree, has been around since ancient times, and from the 1950s patents have been filed for mushroom material to create paper and bandages. Still, Mylo is interesting. The first step is to grow mycelium, the mushroom roots that form a spongy underground web, on sheets of sawdust in a temperature- and humidity-controlled laboratory. Because the rate of growth is two weeks, its carbon footprint is considered exceptionally small. The thick sheets of mycelium are processed, tanned and dyed to create the leather-like fabric that requires only half the volume of water needed for cotton production.

Jamie Bainbridge, Bolt Threads' vice president of product developments, described how the company went through 4,000 versions of Mylo, before finding the right 'suppleness and warmth that genuinely feels natural'.

Stella McCartney's debut collection using Mylo fabric.

PROTEST, RESISTANCE AND SOCIAL MEDIA 2008–PRESENT

'Mylo can be grown in eight to ten days, compared to raising cattle which can take at least eighteen months – and as much as five years,' she added. 'And on its own, in the right conditions, mycelium has the potential to biodegrade.'

McCartney initially created a Mylo version of her Falabella bag for London's Victoria and Albert Museum's Fashioned From Nature exhibit, and in 2020 she teamed up with brands including Adidas and Lululemon to invest in Mylo. In 2021, she launched a black bustier top and trousers made completely from the fabric. It was considered a first step in integrating the fabric into future collections that will eventually play a part in the circular economy. As McCartney noted in a press release, the pieces 'embody our shared commitment with Bolt Threads to innovate a kinder fashion industry – one that sees the birth of beautiful, luxurious materials as opposed to the deaths of our fellow creatures and planet.'

The reaction to McCartney's Mylo couture has been overwhelmingly positive, despite the bustier and utility trousers not immediately being for sale. While she had at first been dismissed for her interest in ethical fashion, other labels are showing an evolving interest in alternative fabrics. It's not just from a concern for the environment and their support of the circular economy – fashion brands realise that to appeal to new consumers they need to tap into the zeitgeist.

'THEY ARE RECOGNIZING THAT THESE COOL MATERIALS OF TOMORROW COULD BE SOMETHING PEOPLE WANT TO BUY TODAY.'

THE NEW YORK TIMES

FASHION AND THE FUTURE – THE CIRCULAR ECONOMY

Over the last several years there has been a movement against the fad for cheaply produced clothing, known as fast fashion, in favour of clothing with a green, sustainable and fair-trade ethos.

With the United Nations estimating that a pair of jeans uses a kilogram of cotton, which requires around 7,500 to 10,000 litres of water to produce, and other reports estimating that the fashion industry accounts for around 10 per cent of global carbon emissions and 20 per cent of waste water, sustainability and environmental consciousness have become more important in fashion in recent years. The interest in ethical fashion coincides with a rise in anti-consumerism and concerns around climate change. Fast fashion is also considered a feminist issue, as cheap, throw-away clothing often exploits factory workers, especially women, in poorer countries.

To combat some of these concerns, the concept of the circular economy has been growing in popularity. It encourages people to reuse and recycle all materials, in order to reduce waste. One report highlighted in Vogue Business, in November 2020, estimated that the potential value of the circular economy in fashion could be worth as much as 5 trillion dollars.

As well as initiatives led by the United Nations Alliance, some clothing companies known for their fast fashion have promised to change their model. H&M, for example, published their plan to run on 100 per cent renewable energy by 2040, and Levi Strauss & Co announced a climate change action plan to reduce greenhouse gas emissions by 40 per cent across its global supply chain by 2025. With the circular economy beginning as a grassroots movement, it shows the power of consumerism in making positive changes for the future.

GLOSSARY

Androgynous: A style of clothing that falls outside of the male and female gender norms.

Art deco: A design style of the 1920s and 1930s which features geometric patterns, stream-lined forms and ornate embellishment. The term derives from the International Exhibition of Modern Decorative and Industrial Arts in Paris in 1925.

Art nouveau: An international decorative art movement which flourished between 1890 and 1910 and is known for its ornamental aesthetics influenced by nature, medieval design and Japanese motifs to create asymmetrical shapes, flowing lines and curved forms.

Atelier: A workshop or studio where a fashion designer creates their designs and fits them to their clients.

Avant-garde: A French term meaning "advance guard", used to describe the spreading of new ideas through innovations in art and culture.

Balaclava: A form of headgear which covers the head and neck, leaving only part of the face exposed. Named after the 1854 Battle of Balaclava during the Crimean War, where British soldiers wore them to keep warm.

Ballets Russes: An influential avant-garde dance company that performed around Europe from 1909 to 1929 and was founded by Sergei Diaghilev.

Bespoke: A term in tailoring in which a pattern is individually measured and created by a skilled cutter for a client, to ensure a perfect fit.

Bias cut: A technique in cutting the fabric diagonally, across the grain, rather than following the straight lines of the weave.

Bloomers: A loose, divided woman's lower garment, which emerged around 1851 and was named after dress reformer Amelia Bloomer.

Boho: Short for 'bohemian', and signifying a relaxed, unconventional form of dress that references nature and eastern cultures to create an individual, unique style.

Chiffon: A light fabric from silk or nylon, which is so thin it's almost transparent.

Circular economy: A model of production and consumption, where clothing is recycled, reused, repaired and shared to ensure there is minimal wastage.

Corset: A support garment designed to be worn under clothing to shape and train the body into a desired shape.

Cotton: A fabric that is made from the fibrous substance of the tropical and subtropical cotton plant.

Couture: The French word for dressmaking, defining a type of clothing which is custom-made for clients.

Crêpe de Chine: A lightweight fabric which has a smooth, matte finish, as opposed to the crimped appearance of crêpe. Traditionally made from silk, it can also be produced from cotton and synthetic materials.

Crinoline: A hooped petticoat worn under a skirt, designed to hold and widen its shape.

Denim: A tough cotton twill fabric, commonly used for jeans. The name is believed to derive from the French town of Nimes, and the phrase *serge de Nimes*.

Fashion blogger: An individual who shares their experiences and ideas on fashion, often using their own image.

Fashion week: Fashion industry event held at key cities around the world, where designers and brands can display their latest collection to buyers and the media.

Fast fashion: The mass-manufacturing of inexpensive clothing by retailers in response to the latest trends.

Fetish-wear: A specialist type of clothing designed to be sexually provocative and deviant in nature. Often made from metal, leather and PVC plastic.

Flapper: A term that originally meant fledgling bird or adolescent girl, before coming to define the new generation of energetic young woman in the 1920s who embraced their freedoms.

Gabardine: A durable twill-woven cloth made from cotton, which is known for its smooth finish. Commonly used for coats, trousers and uniforms.

Glam rock: A rock music movement in the early 1970s where male performers wore flamboyant clothing and make-up for an outrageous sense of style and showmanship.

Goth subculture: An off-shoot of the punk movement, emerging in the late 1970s and noted for the embracing of Victorian aesthetics, the macabre and all-black clothing.

Grunge: A subculture that emerged in the late 1980s and early 1990s in the Pacific Northwest of the United States, where rock bands combined a lumberjack and skateboarder style as an anti-fashion statement.

Haute couture: A French term for exclusive, bespoke dressmaking, meaning 'high-fashion', which is applied to clothing that is made-to-order for private clients, and constructed entirely by hand at an atelier that employs fifteen or more full-time staff.

Heroin Chic: A fashion trend of the early 1990s, which was characterised by thin, pale models who appeared to be undernourished, and which was criticised for its promotion of addiction and unhealthy lifestyles.

High Street fashion: A term for the mass-market, readily available clothing that can be bought from shops on the average UK high street, as opposed to being specially made by designers.

Hip-hop: A culture that emerged in African-American communities in the south Bronx in the early 1970s, which is made up of four tenets – breakdancing, DJing, graffiti and rapping (MCing).

Hoodie: A hooded sweatshirt or jacket, often worn as sportswear, where the hood can be worn over the head or down.

Jersey: A lightweight knit fabric, which was originally made from wool and traditionally produced on the Channel island of Jersey.

Lycra: A brand name for a stretchy elastic polyurethane fibre, popular in sportswear and swimsuits.

Minimalism: A mode of fashion which removes the unnecessary clutter for a simplified, functional aesthetic.

Mod subculture: A fashion-conscious youth culture that began in London in the late 1950s, influenced by European and Ivy League tailoring. Meaning 'modern', the word came to be applied to anything youthful, fun, hip and innovative.

New Wave: Initially a term that defined the post-punk music genre that emerged in the late 1970s, when applied to fashion, it represents a style of dress that incorporates New Romantic, punk and hip-hop styles.

Nylon: A synthetic thermoplastic derived from petroleum and designed to replicate silk.

Off-the-rack: Garments that are available to buy as they are, and which come in a variety of standardised sizes.

Polyester: A synthetic fibre derived from petroleum to create polyethylene terephthalate, first produced in 1941 as a commercial product.

Psychedelia: A fashion and music subculture of the 1960s that references the effects of mind-altering drugs like LSD in its bold, clashing colours and optical illusions.

Punk: A street style that emerged in the early 1970s, combining bondage-wear with rocker fashions of distressed denim and leather, vibrant dyed hair, and accessories like chains, safety-pins and studs.

Ready-to-wear: Known as prêt-à-porter in French, it is the term for garments that are sold as a finished product in a variety of standardised sizes, as opposed to bespoke.

Satin: A type of weave that creates a fabric with a smooth, shiny surface and is made from different fibres, including silk and cotton.

Silhouette: The outline of garments and the shape they make when they hang on the body.

Silk: A luxurious textile made from the threads of the silkworm and produced when forming their cocoons.

Sportswear: Initially an American fashion term for separates in the 1920s, it came to define informal clothing offering comfort and freedom for playing sports.

Street style: Considered to be a grassroots, individual form of dress that is connected with youth culture. Later adapted by fashion bloggers to peacock at fashion week events, combining high-end fashion with an individual twist.

Surrealism: A branch of the avant-garde movement that emerged after World War I and tapped into the potential of the unconscious mind in creating illogical designs with new techniques.

Sustainable fashion: A movement that encourages the fashion industry to adopt ecological and ethical policies.

Tulle: A very fine netting created from silk, cotton or nylon, which was popular for ballet dancer tutus in the nineteenth century.

Tuxedo: A formal black evening suit for men, worn with a white shirt with front panelling, and named after Tuxedo Park, a gathering place for the American elite in Hudson Valley.

Utility fashion: Introduced in 1941 by the British Government during World War II as part of the rationing scheme, in response to a shortage of material. Utility items were considered essential, adaptable and durable.

Vreeland, Diana: The influential French-American editor and writer who was columnist at *Harper's Bazaar* from 1936 to 1962, editor-in-chief at American *Vogue* from 1963 to 1971, and special consultant at the Costume Institute of the Metropolitan Museum of Art from 1971.

Wintour, Anna: British-born editor-in-chief of American *Vogue* since 1988.

Youthquake: A term coined by Diana Vreeland in 1965 to describe the youthful cultural movements of the time.

The publishers would like to thank all those listed below for permission to reproduce the images. Every care has been taken to trace copyright holders. Any copyright holders we have been unable to reach are invited to contact the publishers so that a full acknowledgement may be given in subsequent editions.

p.6 Larry Ellis/Getty;
p.9 Hugo Philpott/Getty;
p.17 Universal History Archive/Getty;
p.21 Mary Evans Picture Library;
p.23, 55, 61 Bettmann/Getty;
p.25 Archivio GBB/Alamy;
pp.27, 77 Hulton Deutsch/Getty;
p.29 IanDagnall Computing/Alamy;
p.31 Granger/Shutterstock; p.35 Eugene Robert Richee/Getty;
p.45 © Cecil Beaton / Victoria and Albert Museum, London;
p.47 Ullstein Bild/Getty;
p.49 Horst P. Horst, Vogue, © Condé Nast;
p.53 'Chicago S 44 (No. 140) Catalog', Box 94, Mongomery Ward records, Collection Number 8088, American Heritage Center, University of Wyoming;
p.55 George Hurrell/Getty;
p.57 John Kisch Archives/Getty;
p.63 Fred Ramage/Getty;
p.65 Kammerman/Getty;
p.67 Chicago History Museum/Getty;
p.75 H. Armstrong Roberts/ClassicStock/Getty;
pp.81, 83, 109 Mirrorpix/Getty;
p.85 Everett/Shutterstock;
p.89 Keystone/Getty;
p.91 Reg Lancaster/Getty;
p.93 United Archives/Getty;
p.97 Justin de Villeneuve/Getty;
p.99, 125 Michael Ochs Archives/Getty;
pp.101, 117 Daniel Simon/Getty;
p.105 Granger/Alamy;
p.111 PA Images/Alamy;
p.113 Virginia Turbett/Getty;
p.115 Images Press/Getty;
p.127 Janette Beckman/Getty;
p.129 Gie Knaeps/Getty;
pp.131, 157 Retro AdArchives/Alamy;
p.133 Paul Massey/Shutterstock;
p.135 Dan Lecca, Vogue, © Condé Nast;
pp.139, 151 © Firstview/IMAXtree.com;
p.141 Yoshikazu Tsuno/Getty;
p.143 Gareth Davies/Getty;
p.145 Ron Galella/Getty;
p.147 Ken Towner/ANL/Shutterstock;
p.153 © Shoichi Aoki;
p.155 Ron Davis/Getty;
p.159 Pierre Verdy/Getty;
p.169 Kevin Winter/Getty;
p.171 courtesy of Dossier Journal, photo © Collier Schorr;
p.173 Zacharie Scheurer/AP/Shutterstock;
p.175 Jacopo M. Raule/Getty;
p.179; p.181 Fernando Leon/Getty;
p.183 Jim West/Alamy;
p.185 Wayne Tippetts/Shutterstock;
p.189 L Ben Hider/Getty, R Daniel Zuchnik;
p.191 Slaven Vlasic/Getty;
p.193 courtesy of Columbia;
p.195 © Stella McCartney.

INDEX

CULTURE QUAKE

A bold new series charting popular
culture's most disruptive, rebellious
and ground breaking works.

ARTQUAKE:
THE MOST DISRUPTIVE WORKS
IN MODERN ART
Susie Hodge

FASHIONQUAKE:
THE MOST DISRUPTIVE MOMENTS
IN FASHION
Caroline Young

FILMQUAKE:
THE MOST DISRUPTIVE FILMS
IN CINEMA
Ian Haydn Smith

MUSICQUAKE:
THE MOST DISRUPTIVE MOMENTS
IN MUSIC
Robert Dimery